AFTER THE NEW ATHEIST DEBATE

The first decade of the twenty-first century saw a number of best-selling books which not only challenged the existence of god, but claimed that religious faith was dangerous and immoral. The New Atheists, as writers such as Richard Dawkins, Christopher Hitchens, Sam Harris, and Daniel Dennett have become known, sparked a vicious debate over religion's place in modern society.

In *After the New Atheist Debate*, Phil Ryan offers both an elegant summary of this controversy and a path out of the cul-de-sac that this argument has become. Drawing on the social sciences, philosophy, and theology, Ryan examines the claims of the New Atheists and of their various religious and secular opponents and finds both sides wanting.

Rather than the mutual demonization that marks the New Atheist debate, Ryan argues that modern society needs respectful ethical dialogue in which citizens present their points of view and seek to understand the positions of others. Lucidly written and clearly argued, *After the New Atheist Debate* is a book that brings welcome clarity and a solid path to the often contentious conversation about religion in the public sphere.

PHIL RYAN is an associate professor in the School of Public Policy and Administration at Carleton University. His most recent book, *Multicultiphobia*, was shortlisted for the Canada Prize in the Social Sciences in 2011.

UTP Insights

UTP Insights is an innovative collection of brief books offering accessible introductions to the ideas that shape our world. Each volume in the series focuses on a contemporary issue, offering a fresh perspective anchored in contemporary scholarship. Spanning a broad range of disciplines in the social sciences and humanities, the books in the UTP Insights series will set the agenda for public discourse and debate, as well as provide valuable resources for students and instructors.

BOOKS IN THE SERIES

- Paul M. Evans, *Engaging China: Myth, Aspiration, and Strategy in Canadian Policy from Trudeau to Harper*
- Phil Ryan, *After the New Atheist Debate*

AFTER THE NEW ATHEIST DEBATE

Phil Ryan

UNIVERSITY OF TORONTO PRESS
Toronto Buffalo London

© University of Toronto Press 2014
Toronto Buffalo London
www.utppublishing.com
Printed in the U.S.A.

ISBN 978-1-4426-4952-1 (cloth)
ISBN 978-1-4426-2687-4 (paper)

Printed on acid-free, 100% post-consumer recycled paper with vegetable-based inks.

Library and Archives Canada Cataloguing in Publication

Ryan, Phil, author
After the new atheist debate/Phil Ryan.

(UTP insights)
Includes bibliographical references.
ISBN 978-1-4426-4952-1 (bound). – ISBN 978-1-4426-2687-4 (pbk.)

1. Atheism.   2. Christianity and atheism.   I. Title.   II. Series: UTP insights

BL2747.3.R93 2014   211'.8   C2014-905021-6

University of Toronto Press acknowledges the financial assistance to its publishing program of the Canada Council for the Arts and the Ontario Arts Council, an agency of the Government of Ontario.

 Canada Council Conseil des Arts
for the Arts du Canada

ONTARIO ARTS COUNCIL
CONSEIL DES ARTS DE L'ONTARIO
an Ontario government agency
un organisme du gouvernement de l'Ontario

University of Toronto Press acknowledges the financial support of the Government of Canada through the Canada Book Fund for its publishing activities.

For John and Aidan,

My philosophers-in-residence

Much political debate betrays the marks of warfare. It consists in rallying the troops and intimidating the other side, which must now increase its efforts or back down. In all this one may find the thought that to have character is to have firm convictions and be ready to proclaim them defiantly to others. To be is to confront.

John Rawls

Contents

Scriptural Abbreviations

Biblical quotations use the Revised Standard Version.

1 Cor	1 Corinthians
1 Jn	1 John
1 Pet	1 Peter
1 Sam	1 Samuel
1 Tim	1 Timothy
2 Pet	2 Peter
2 Sam	2 Samuel
2 Tim	2 Timothy
Deut	Deuteronomy
Eccles	Ecclesiastes
Gal	Galatians
Heb	Hebrews
Is	Isaiah
Jn	John
Job	Job
Mt	Matthew
Phil	Philippians
Prov	Proverbs
Ps	Psalms
Rom	Romans
Sir	Sirach*

* = Deuterocanonical book

AFTER THE NEW ATHEIST DEBATE

Introduction

The fight over evolution has reached the big, big screen. Several Imax theaters, including some in science museums, are refusing to show movies that mention the subject – or the Big Bang or the geology of the earth – fearing protests from people who object to films that contradict biblical descriptions of the origin of Earth and its creatures.

Dean (2005)

Rep. Katherine Harris (R-Fla.) said this week that God did not intend for the United States to be a "nation of secular laws" and that the separation of church and state is a "lie we have been told" to keep religious people out of politics. "If you're not electing Christians, then in essence you are going to legislate sin," Harris told interviewers.

Stratton (2006)

Reports of the religious climate at the Air Force Academy are unsettling: A chaplain instructs cadets to try to convert classmates by warning that they "will burn in the fires of hell" if they do not accept Christ. During basic training, freshman cadets who decline to attend after-dinner chapel are marched back to their dormitories in "heathen flights" organized by upperclassmen. A Jewish student is taunted as a Christ killer and told that the Holocaust was the just punishment for that offense. The academy's head football coach posts a banner in the locker room that proclaims, "I am a Christian first and last ... I am a member of Team Jesus Christ."

Washington Post (4 June 2005)

A jury heard a recording yesterday of the last frenzied, despairing moments of Flight 93, as passengers stormed the cockpit to prevent hijackers from crashing the United Airlines plane into its presumed target, the US Capitol, on 11 September 2001. "Shall we finish it off?" the voice of one of the hijackers asks, amid sounds of a desperate struggle as the plane was about to begin its plunge into a Pennsylvania field. "Pull it down, pull it down," says another voice, in what appear to be the final instructions to send UA93 to its doom. Then there is heard only repeated cries of "Allah is the greatest, Allah is the greatest," before the 32-minute tape ends.

Cornwell (2006)

India's increasingly nationalistic government is rewriting school text books to depict Muslims and Christians as alien villains ... An examination question in the state of Uttar Pradesh asked: "If it takes four savaks [Hindu religious workers] to demolish one mosque, how many does it take to demolish 20?"

Bates (2000)

Religion in the news does not represent the whole truth about religion in the world. Most believers don't make the news: they lead quiet lives, shaped to a greater or lesser degree by religious beliefs that often help make them more caring and committed people. But while these grim news articles provide a one-sided picture of religion, they do not constitute a simple fabrication.

No one should have been surprised, then, when a series of provocative and lively attacks on religion was published in the wake of the 9/11 attacks and the rise of a politically assertive conservative Christianity. Six works give us a fair picture of the genre:

– Sam Harris, *The End of Faith* (2004), and *Letter to a Christian Nation* (2006);
– Richard Dawkins, *The God Delusion* (2006);
– Daniel Dennett, *Breaking the Spell* (2006);
– Christopher Hitchens, *God Is Not Great: How Religion Poisons Everything* (2007); and
– Michel Onfray, *In Defence of Atheism* (2007).

These writers have been dubbed the "New Atheists." I will use the label, though it is not a perfect fit. Their achievement is to "say very old things in a new way," to borrow a phrase (Gilson 1937, 59).

They share a name. Yet the New Atheists differ in their ostensible goals. Only Harris explicitly seeks the "eradication" of religion (2006, 87). Hitchens holds out no such hope: "Religious faith is, precisely *because* we are still-evolving creatures, ineradicable." So Hitchens seeks merely to limit religion's power to coerce him or anyone else: he asks to be *left alone* (2007, 12–13).[1] Onfray agrees that religion is here to stay: "A fiction does not die, an illusion never passes away." So he wishes to put us on guard against the many pathologies of religion, through a "deconstruction" of "the three monotheisms," of "Christianity in particular," and of "theocracy." But Onfray wishes to take a further step, one that distinguishes him from the other New Atheists: "Atheism is not an end in itself," but a vital step to "Another morality, a new ethic" (2007, 12, 59, 34). Dennett, for his part, claims not to oppose religion. He merely wishes to break an alleged taboo against its objective study: "I want to put religion on the examination table. If it is fundamentally benign, as many of its devotees insist, it should emerge just fine" (2006, 39).[2] Dawkins, finally, is seeking to "raise consciousness." His book is structured around various "consciousness-raising messages": "You can be an atheist who is happy, balanced, moral, and intellectually fulfilled," for example, or "A proper understanding of the magnificence of the real world" can meet our need for inspiration (2006, 1, 3). And the goal of his consciousness-raising? "If this book works as I intend, religious readers who open it will be atheists when they put it down" (5).

I am a Christian, yet I find much to agree with in these works. The Bible and other sacred scriptures have certainly been used to justify barbarity. Organized religions have been complicit with tyranny, oppression, even genocide. Treating the Bible as a science text is indeed a recipe for ignorance. Expecting political candidates to make public professions of faith corrupts democracy (and religion, for that matter). That said, these books may exacerbate many of the problems they identify. No realistic observer thinks that religion is going to vanish from this earth any time soon. If one is concerned about the dangerous effects of religion, then, two strategies are worth pursuing. One is to strengthen "nontoxic" forms of religion (or, if you prefer, "less toxic" forms), relative to the more toxic variants. The other is to clarify the proper place of religion in a modern democracy, through ongoing dialogue. Both of these paths are undermined by many aspects of the New Atheists' books.

Despite occasional protestations to the contrary, the New Atheists do not view non-fundamentalist belief as worthy of serious consideration. Harris declares that he is considering only "Christianity in its most committed forms." His "committed" Christian believes, among other things, that all non-Christians are hellbound (2006, ix, viii). For Hitchens, "true" belief is domineering and intolerant: "The true believer cannot rest until the whole world bows the knee" (2007, 31). Dawkins insists that *all* belief "discourages questioning, by its very nature." Hence, "the teachings of 'moderate' religion, though not extremist in themselves, are an open invitation to extremism." The problem for Dawkins is "religion itself, not religious *extremism* – as though that were some kind of terrible perversion of real, decent religion" (2006, 306). Dennett, finally, views movements away from the simplest religious views as clever stratagems designed to shield belief from critical challenge. He is particularly suspicious of the very idea of religious tolerance. What are we to make of those who "call themselves religious" yet advocate tolerance, he asks. One possibility is that they have no serious commitment to any particular religion. But there is also a "Machiavellian" possibility: the believer who claims to be tolerant simply realizes that "the time is not ripe for candid declarations of religious superiority" (2006, 290).

So what? Is there any cost to this approach other than the ruffled feathers of religious "moderates"? There is. We will see that the New Atheists do not really expect to persuade the "true" believers who are the principal target of their denunciations. Yet they dismiss precisely those believers who might be willing to engage them in a respectful dialogue. Rather than initiating an ongoing dialogue, then, the New Atheists are out to "rally the troops," to draw sharp lines between sane and sophisticated unbelievers and the religious rubes who surround them, to help atheists feel good about themselves.[3] One of the dangers of this stance, as we shall see throughout this book, is to present as religious pathologies what are in fact more general aspects of the human condition.

1. The New Atheist Debate

Their focus on rallying the troops suggests that the New Atheists are writing primarily for fellow unbelievers. But many believers have been paying attention as well, and have been moved to write replies. Whatever the original goals of the New Atheists, a debate of sorts is thus under way. The New Atheist debate is not a simple two-sided affair. Harris, Dawkins, & Co. represent one party to the debate. But those who oppose them do not form a single camp. We have, among others: fundamentalists such as Douglas Wilson and Theodore Beale,[4] more traditional "mainstream" Christians, including John Haught and Alister McGrath, conservative Catholics such as Thomas Crean and Michael Novak, left-leaning agnostic Chris Hedges, and even Marxist theorist Terry Eagleton. For simplicity's sake, however, I will often speak of the "two sides" in this debate. Rather than continually refer to "those who have written replies to the New Atheists," I will label these various writers "the defenders," as they answer the "prosecution" charges presented by the New Atheists.[5]

The New Atheist debate can be examined from different angles. The most obvious one is theological: how strong are the arguments presented for or against God's existence, for or against the reasonableness of belief and unbelief? This aspect naturally seems of greatest importance to most participants in the debate. But we can bypass this dimension of the debate: the existence and nature of God is a matter on which the respectful coexistence of many perspectives is entirely possible, as we find in most developed societies today.[6]

There is, though, a dimension to the debate that we cannot avoid. We might term this the political dimension. It concerns questions such as: How are we to live together? What is the place of religion in a modern democracy? To what extent should democratic laws constrain religious freedom? What are the ethical principles that a community should embody in law? Such questions cannot be avoided. Answers can be imposed by a ruthless majority (which may become tomorrow's minority), or they can be worked out in a respectful ongoing dialogue. But to enjoy such a dialogue, we must move *beyond* the New Atheist debate.

Why? Consider the qualities of a fruitful debate. The parties may reach an agreement. Even without agreement, each side may come to understand the elements of truth in the other's position, and perhaps modify its own position so as to make it more reasonable and tolerant. Even when a debate does not reach agreement, it is a step forward when the parties are freed from the dogmatic assumption that anyone with common sense must think as they do. A visible marker of fruitful debate is *movement* in the parties' positions. This need not be movement towards an "average" of the various positions. But there is movement. This involves another quality: people are able to separate their current positions from their egos. They do not ruthlessly defend their opening stance, fearful that any change would be a sign of defeat or an admission that they were mistaken all along.

Debates, as we all know, are not always so positive. Everyone can get dug into their positions. People seem to be discussing, but they are not really trying to make sense of their opponent's arguments. They listen only in order to *catch* their opponent. They impose the worst possible interpretation on the opponent's words, words seen merely as potential occasions to *pounce*. Each side is increasingly convinced the other's position is stupid or even evil.

The evidence to date suggests that the New Atheist debate has not been a good one. Barriers to understanding are built into its very foundations. The New Atheists portray believers as simpletons, hostile to reason and prone to anger and violence when their dogma is questioned. This portrait determines the New Atheists' typical reaction to critiques of their work. Dawkins characterizes responses to the New Atheist manifestos as "fluttering in the dovecots of the deluded" (2007). His website, richarddawkins.net, dismisses those who have responded to his *God Delusion* as "fleas."

Dennett responds to a scathing *New York Times* review (Wieseltier 2006) of his *Breaking the Spell* by suggesting that the reviewer was probably "deathly afraid" (2007).

Many of the defenders have answered in kind. Beale fulminates against "the fraudulent, error-filled writings" of the New Atheists (2008, 2).[7] Feser declares that "atheist chic" has "lost all inhibition, by turns blaspheming, whoring, and otherwise offending against all sane and decent sensibilities" (2008, viii). Berlinski mocks the "poodle-like perplexity" of his opponents (2008, 34). D.B. Hart sneers at Dawkins's "embarrassing incapacity for philosophical reasoning" (2009, 4), and Alvin Plantinga concurs: to call Dawkins's philosophizing "sophomoric," he declares, "would be unfair to sophomores" (2009, 248).[8]

Tellingly, many participants in the New Atheist debate wield the language, not of dialogue, but of battle. Onfray writes cryptically of the need to prepare for the "wars ahead" (2007, 218). Harris announces that he is out to "arm" those "who believe that religion should be kept out of public policy" (2004, viii). Responding in kind, Feser declares that "secularism ought to be driven back into the intellectual and political margins whence it came" (2008, x), Beale solemnly proclaims his book an "intellectual deathmatch" (2008, 3), and Dinesh D'Souza announces that we are in the midst of "a war over religion, and it has been declared by leading Western atheists who have commenced hostilities," sternly warning those Christians who might be inclined to make nice: "This is not a time for Christians to turn the other cheek. Rather, it is a time to drive the money-changers out of the temple" (2007, xv).[9]

Some of the defenders even stoop to the suggestion that their opponents are enemies of society itself. Beale alleges that Harris "attacks religious faith because it stands in the way of his dream of the ultimate destruction of America" (2008, 116). Serious charges require serious evidence, but Beale offers none at all. Feser declares the "secularist" creed to be "a clear and present danger to the stability of any society" (2008, xi). "Clear and present danger" alludes to Supreme Court Justice Holmes's test for the legitimacy of restraints on free speech.[10] Is Feser truly suggesting that "secularist" speech ought to be banned?

Not all contributions to the New Atheist debate have adopted this shrill tone. David Myers's *A Friendly Letter to Skeptics and Atheists* offers a careful answer to many aspects of the New Atheist critique, one that acknowledges "considerable common ground" between his more liberal Christianity and the New Atheists (2008, v). The short debate between Daniel Dennett and Alister McGrath was also admirably civil (2008).

Honourable exceptions aside, many of the writings that have dominated the New Atheist debate are saturated with anger, hatred, contempt, and fear. Honest dialogue cannot take place under the sway of such emotions. To this, many of the leading participants in the debate will respond with a shrug: who cares about debate when your opponents are evil, stupid, or both? The question suggests its own answer: we need to dialogue, precisely so that we might learn that our opponents are neither evil nor stupid.

Apart from the futility of the debate itself, there is another cost to the New Atheist debate. To the extent that it polarizes, that it confirms each side in a negative view of the other, the debate can contribute to the polarization of democracy itself. "Logically," says Thomas Crean, "the atheist must be shameless, that is, inhuman" (2007, 157). Moved by a similar spirit of tolerance, Dawkins dismisses the "Bible Belt" as America's "reptilian brain" (2007), and professes to be mystified that anyone "worthy of the name of sophisticated" can be a Christian (2006, 60). So how can the righteous accept rule by the "shameless"? How can the mature and enlightened respect government by the "reptilian"? It is reasonable to expect anyone who really absorbs the venom from one side or another of the New Atheist debate to end up declaring: "Rule by the people, all right; but we cannot accept rule by this lot, because we are not part of their people," as philosopher Charles Taylor once put it (1999, 268). Such division is not easily healed: "When water chokes, what is one to wash it down with?," asked Aristotle (*Ethics* 1146a). When debate itself polarizes, what resources for reconciliation remain?

Clearly, many people today are unconcerned by polarization. They are in the grip of a fantasy: that they can live in isolation from those they hate, that they can spend their time communing with like-minded people, nursing their shared sense of superiority, nursing their contempt for those who are different, never accepting that there is only one world, a world in which all must live and reason together. "All I ask of the apostle Paul is that he and his followers and emulators leave me alone," pleads Hitchens (Hitchens and Wilson 2008, 36). "All the vast majority of the billions of people of faith on the planet ask," answers Beale, "is to be left alone to believe what we choose to believe and to live how we decide to live" (2008, 6).

This is a dangerous fantasy. We cannot simply "leave each other alone." What some people mean by "leave me alone," first, often requires that others shut up, not fight for their rights, not express their opinions. Recall our news story about the Air Force Academy: when some members of Congress tried to ban coercive religious proselytizing there, the move was denounced by a Republican Congressman as part of "the long war on Christianity in America" (Allen 2005). The same overheated rhetoric opens David Aikman's *Delusion of Disbelief*: "A great assault upon faith was launched in 2006 against unsuspecting Americans." What was this "great assault?" The publication of "three books by atheists" (Aikman 2008, 1). Leave each other alone? We can't: even a modest goal such as "peaceful coexistence" can only be attained through dialogue. And it is far too modest a goal. Like it or not, we do not simply coexist: we have joint responsibility for our society, and for our world.

2. This Book

Despite the New Atheist debate's shortcomings, it has served to increase the public profile of beliefs that millions of people already shared. Many atheists, after all, were certain that believers are credulous, neurotic, and prone to violence, long before the New Atheists made this claim. Indeed, this probably accounts for the high sales of New Atheist works, which served to confirm many readers in their views. Conversely, many believers already viewed atheists as profoundly immoral, even dangerous, and resented the idea of a democratic society in which they must respectfully interact with atheists.[11] Thus, despite its noxious qualities, the New Atheist debate has brought to the surface opinions that are worth discussing.

While this book critiques the debate, it is *not* about one of the central issues in that debate: whether it is reasonable to believe in God. As noted above, we can live happily together in society, even in a single household, and disagree on that question. But there are other matters that we must discuss in order to live together, and this book calls for respectful dialogue on those matters.

Because this book takes up various points of contention in the New Atheist debate from a different angle than that of its leading protagonists, I should say a word about a point of view that shapes the work. Nearly all the leading voices on both sides of the New Atheist debate assume that *we do what we do because we believe what we believe*. Thus, a recurring theme of the New Atheists is that believers do bad things precisely *because* of their beliefs. One sign of Sam Harris's belief in the potency of belief is his claim that "some propositions are so dangerous that it may even be ethical to kill people for believing them" (2004, 52). Harris is so convinced on this point that he dismisses the claim that "the Islamic doctrines of martyrdom and jihad are not the cause of Islamic terrorism" as one of the "most dishonest religious apologies I have ever heard" (2010, 23).[12]

Michel Onfray follows the same approach. After running through various verses of the Koran that describe Paradise, Onfray concludes: "How natural that Palestinian suicide bombers should unleash death on Israeli café terraces; that aircraft hijackers should hurl passenger planes against New York's Twin Towers; that Islamic radicals should detonate a string of powerful bombs on packed commuter trains in Madrid" (2007, 101). Various New Atheists attribute a further mysterious power to ideas, that of *contamination*. This metaphor, which we will examine in chapter 5, is found in various forms in Dawkins, Dennett, Hitchens, and Onfray.

Many of the defenders, on the other hand, paint a picture of inevitable moral decline should the influence of religion in the world wane. Michael Novak, for example, claims that secularism has led society to "moral carelessness": "We remember nostalgically a time when one could leave home with the door unlocked" (2008, 268). To a large degree they play the same game as the New Atheists, but simply reverse its sign: good things flow from belief, bad things flow out of unbelief.

This viewpoint that dominates the New Atheist debate has often been called "idealism." Its obvious implication is that beliefs are a vital pressure point in the world, through which much else can be transformed. It thus inflates the importance of the New Atheist debate itself, whose leading voices insist that the world would be a much better place if it could rid itself of whichever ideas they themselves dislike.

One influential alternative to idealism simply reverses the direction of causality. In Marx's famous formulation, "It is not the consciousness of men that determines their existence, but their social existence that determines their consciousness" (rpt. 1969, 1: 503). Marx and Engels themselves termed this alternative "materialism," a confusing term today, given its other meanings.

By contrast, the approach that shapes this work does not simply reverse idealism's causal claim. Its guiding postulate is that both actions and beliefs are *shaped* (not determined) by our life in society. Moreover, while this life can sometimes act directly on our beliefs, and through our beliefs indirectly on our actions, it can also shape our actions directly, which in turn reshape our beliefs. That is, as we make our way through life, we seek some degree of harmony between what we believe and what we do. To attain this, sometimes we shape our actions according to our beliefs, sometimes we do the reverse. Action is not a moon orbiting the planet of belief. Action and belief circle each other, under the influence of our social milieux, and these milieux are over time reshaped by our actions and beliefs. Thus, the approach followed here does not deny that beliefs can influence actions.[13] But it does not ascribe a primordial status to our beliefs. It highlights something that the idealist *also* knows, but does not sufficiently take into account: our beliefs *come* from somewhere, and we ourselves are always already actors somewhere in the world when we choose, consciously or not, whether to embrace particular ideas, how seriously to take them, and so on.

Because this approach gives great importance to social context for understanding beliefs and action, I will label it the "social view." To work within the social view does not mean that one works only with the social sciences. The latter have an important contribution to make, yet they have no monopoly on the social view. Theologians, for example, have often examined the ways in which religious doctrines, and even religious scriptures themselves, were consciously and unconsciously shaped by social influences. Such an approach need not deny that doctrines have *also* been shaped by an ongoing process of reflection and systematization.

As understood here, the social view is modest, avoiding strong but controversial positions that would deflect attention from its basic insights. Thus, it takes no position on the "nature-nurture" question, and certainly does not posit a "blank slate" (Pinker 2002). It is not determinist, nor is it "perfectionist," believing that some "adequate pedagogical technique will finally produce the 'socialised man' and thus solve the problems of society" (Niebuhr 1960, 24).

Yet the social view insists that we are thrown into a social world not of our choosing, a social world that shapes us intimately. "History does not belong to us," as philosopher Hans-Georg Gadamer puts it; "we belong to it" (1989, 276). That is, much of what we believe reflects the particular fragment of history in which we find ourselves, the times and places in which we happen to have lived. We do not enjoy sole authorship of our identity.[14]

3. Plan of the Work

Part One of this book examines the New Atheist debate from various angles. Chapter 1 opens with an overview of the New Atheist charges against religion. Religion, we are told, promotes violence and stupidity, divides humanity, supports tyranny, and is generally meddlesome and power-hungry. The chapter will then critique various quick answers offered by the defenders, such as the claim that the New Atheists grossly misrepresent Christian faith.

Chapter 2 wrestles with the claim that religion has been "the most prolific source of violence in our history," as Sam Harris puts it. The chapter begins by considering a common response to such claims: religion is a mere pretext for the evil committed in its name. "Piety is the mask," claimed philosopher William James, but "the inner force is tribal instinct" (rpt. 1999, 370). The defenders also counter the attacks on religion by pointing to the history of twentieth-century atheist totalitarianism, to which the New Atheists respond: totalitarianism was not atheist. Nazism, they argue, was a Christian phenomenon, a claim that will require a brief examination of the relation between Christians and the Nazi movement. Even Stalinism or the Khmer Rouge, it is argued, manifested many of the traits of religion. But to make a monk out of Stalin or a priest out of Pol Pot, the New Atheism does two things: it considerably stretches the concept of religion, and it divides humanity itself into two camps, those who cling to unwarranted belief, and those who "live by evidence." This requires two problematic assumptions: that *anyone* can entirely "live by evidence," and that "reason" and science can deliver us from all manner of evil. Both assumptions will be challenged.

Chapter 3 examines the New Atheist debate's duelling caricatures. What image would one have of believers, if everything one knew about them was drawn from the works of the New Atheists? And what would one think of atheists, if one had met them only in the pages of the defenders? The New Atheists tell us that believers are infantile, dogmatic, stupid, dishonest, violent, and intolerant. Unbelievers are a different matter altogether: mature and psychologically healthy, open-minded, better educated, more moral, courageous, and non-violent. Various defenders respond in kind. Atheists are in the grip of a world view that is immoral, even insane. They are morally corrupt, and often embrace atheism to give free reign to their corruption. When they get their hands on political power, they are often genocidal. The chapter critiques these duelling caricatures, and points to some of their underlying similarities. It also examines what I call the "geography of belief and unbelief," a reality obscured by the caricatures, and one that shows how misleading it can be to talk of belief and unbelief as abstract unchanging phenomena.

Unfair stereotypes, however, tend to be resilient. A nasty caricature of the "others" provides one with good motives to avoid those others, distrust their arguments, ignore disconfirming evidence and focus on information favourable to one's prejudices. Various supporting beliefs also protect stereotypes against inconvenient facts. Chapter 4 tackles one of the most effective supporting beliefs: the distinction between the "true" believer or atheist and those who are "wishy-washy." The New Atheists grant that many believers are not notably violent or intolerant. But that is simply because they are not *true* believers. Unlike the true believers, they do not take their sacred scriptures seriously, which for the New Atheists means that they do not read scripture literally. One becomes moderate, reasonable, and tolerant, precisely to the extent that one strays from the path of belief. Defenders offer an analogous argument: yes, some atheists seem like reasonable and moral people, but that is simply because they have failed to follow their own world view to its logical conclusion. They are moral parasites, unconsciously borrowing their ethics from the believers around them. The true "hard core" atheist, by contrast, cannot be moral, having lost all possible moral foundations.

Such supporting claims are harder to refute than simple caricatures. Chapter 4 will address the New Atheist vision of the "true" believer. (The corresponding claim concerning the "true" atheist will be addressed in later chapters, when we discuss the idea of moral foundations.) The chapter argues that violence is as likely to arise from uncertainty and fear as from theological certainty. A rigid religious certainty, far from being the motor of violence, may be its by-product: since beliefs often flow from actions, violence can generate the certainty that justifies it. And as much violence today is sponsored by violent organizations, we need to understand the reciprocal influence of belief and action as a person becomes more deeply involved in such an organization. The New Atheists' related assumption, that serious faith demands a literal approach to scripture, reflects a misunderstanding of Christian history, a misunderstanding shared by many modern Christians. This is not a point of theology, but of historical record: as the chapter will show, Christians throughout history have not read the Bible literally.

But why would non-Christian readers be interested in matters such as the history of Christian approaches to the Bible? Has the argument not turned excessively "intra-mural" at this point? No. It is clear today that widely shared biblical interpretations have so-cial and political implications for everyone. No matter what one's metaphysical orientation, it is helpful to know that Christianity has not been characterized by scriptural literalism throughout its history. Knowing this, one need never allow Bible-based moral or political claims to be "conversation-stoppers" (Rorty 1999, 171).

Part Two takes up a central question of the New Atheist debate, the challenge of identifying and supporting the ethics with which we are to live together. Chapter 5 examines New Atheist views on post-religious ethics. I pay particular attention to Sam Harris's at-tempt to develop an ethical "science," as he is the most explicit of the New Atheists on ethical matters. While dialogue is in principle open to anyone, science is a matter for experts. Thus, a new scien-tific ethics is to be worked out only by "those who are adequate to the task," as Harris puts it. But Harris's efforts carry him in some disturbing directions. His "scientific" system of ethics approves of torture, even of innocent people, and is open to a nuclear first strike on a civilian population. One might attribute these conclu-sions to the failings of an individual thinker, but none of the other New Atheists objects to Harris's ethical arguments. Indeed, their own ethical musings also provide serious cause for concern, as we will see.

The New Atheists' failure to present a plausible post-religious ethics would seem to support the view that morality requires a reli-gious foundation. This is the defenders' central claim. It is the basis for the assertion that atheism is an *inherently* immoral world view, and that the *consistent* atheist must be a monster. Chapter 6 argues, however, that religious belief itself cannot provide us with a shared ethical foundation. At first blush, this claim will strike many be-lievers as absurd. But I take it as given that we live in a pluralistic society, and I stipulate that a shared ethical foundation would be recognizable as such to all reasonable people willing to inquire diligently into ethical questions. Understood this way, we can see that "biblical morality," or some more sophisticated version of reli-gious ethics, cannot give our society a firm ethical foundation. The chapter shows, in particular, that the arguments advanced by the defenders to demonstrate that unbelievers lack ethical grounding can easily be turned against the defenders' own claims.

Chapter 7 generalizes the finding of the previous chapter, advancing the falsifiable claim that no shared ethical foundations are available to us. It points, moreover, to serious dangers associated with the view that any morality without foundations is subjective and arbitrary. Our lack of shared foundations does *not* leave us with moral chaos or nihilism. Rather, we are left with the imperfect world in which we in fact live, a world in which we face a contradictory welter of normative demands aimed at us from a variety of sources, demands to which we respond for a variety of nonfoundational reasons. Each of us individually, and all of us together, thus face the task of identifying the *oughts* that are truly worthy of our respect.

The analysis suggests that a just and humane society must sort out, develop, defend, and transmit its moral world. It will do this in part through ongoing ethical dialogue, which we examine in chapter 8. The chapter argues that such dialogue cannot put all our norms to the test: any particular dialogue subjects just some norms to scrutiny, and must take other existing norms as given in order to do so. The chapter also considers whether "faith-based" arguments may be put forth in all contexts. I will argue that, while society needs broad-based dialogue in which all arguments can be put on the table, there are specific spheres in which we must exercise argumentative restraint. The chapter will conclude by addressing the temptation to avoid broad dialogue through real or psychological withdrawal from "mainstream" society.

Finally, the Conclusion asks "Is this enough?" Can our existing welter of norms, our various non-foundational reasons for respecting norms, and a relatively modest practice of ethical dialogue, save us from chaos? Can it give us the "ethical fibre" we will need to meet future challenges?

4. A Word to Specialists

At the outset of his *Democracy and Tradition*, Jeffrey Stout declares that his book "addresses readers in their capacity as citizens. It seeks a public, as opposed to a narrowly professional, audience"

(2004, 5). Stout was politely pleading with his specialist readers to cut him a bit of slack. I must do the same. To write for citizens, particularly on a theme such as this, one must draw widely. One must "put gates through fences," the fences erected between disciplines (Lovejoy 1964, 16). If you consult the bibliography, you will see that I have wandered far from my disciplinary home in political science. Of the specialist in disciplines where I have trespassed, I ask that you read in a spirit of interdisciplinary tolerance. But what does this mean, exactly? An opportunistic pragmatist might say: "We see your intellectual tradition as just another toolbox, and we will draw on those tools whenever we must, and however we wish. This may upset you, just as a lover of classical music might be miffed to hear Beethoven's Ode to Joy used as a ring tone, but that's just misplaced possessiveness: Beethoven, and your traditions of thought, are in the public domain." One obvious danger of this stance is that the opportunist may be appropriating a "tool" that is already obsolete. Particular insights can be dragged in to build one's argument, a "glib superficial poaching" (Bernstein 1989, 15) unconcerned with how well those insights have fared when exposed to critical scrutiny within their home discipline.

A further problem with this opportunistic approach is suggested by Michael Polanyi's insight that the tools of the mind differ from those of the body. While we can pick up a physical tool and put it down again, we can only use our intellectual framework "by dwelling in it" (1962, 195). Moreover, our framework is not fully accessible to us: "We have no clear knowledge of what our presuppositions are" (59). This suggests a different metaphor: the ideas with which we have worked for some time are akin to our native language, shaping our lived world. In the way that "language speaks us" (Gadamer 1989, 463), so too our intellectual frameworks *create* us to some extent. We come to another discipline or intellectual tradition, then, as adults trying to learn a new language. We can acquire much of its vocabulary, long before we gain comfort with its colloquialisms, its shifting terrain, and its rules of "decorum," rules that indicate which forms of language are to be deployed in which contexts. Even after we master much of that more difficult terrain, we may never learn to think *and dream* in our new language.

Now the rules of decorum of a language or culture are not "frills," as we find out when they seem to change too rapidly or evaporate altogether. Yet we try to have tolerance for the stranger who is not fully familiar with our folkways, mindful perhaps that she is doing her best to make her way through "a land full of traps" (Tocqueville 1986, 2: 242). Our tolerance does not reflect a belief that the rules are trivial and dispensable. They are important, and yet we accept *in the name of other goods* the stranger who does not fully grasp them.

And so for the specialist to read as a citizen is, first, to have that same "multicultural" tolerance of the stranger from another discipline.[15] The second need is for patience when I explain the seemingly obvious. Any interdisciplinary work must "explain certain matters which, to those especially conversant with that province, will need no explanation – but which may not be equally known to specialists in other fields, or to the general reader" (Lovejoy 1964, ix). Any specialist can expect to find styles of thought invoked in this work with which they are not familiar. On the other hand, they will find points made, sometimes at length, in idioms that they do master. The biblical scholar, for example, may find it astonishing that the argument developed in chapter 4 concerning biblical literalism even needs to be stated. But specialists should never overestimate the degree of understanding of their particular area of expertise throughout society as a whole.[16]

part one

The New Atheist Debate

chapter one

Charges and Defence: An Overview

This chapter offers an initial overview of the New Atheist debate. We begin with an inventory of the New Atheist critiques of religion, and then consider some of the more straightforward rebuttals offered by the defenders. Recall, however, the delimitation noted in the introduction: this overview of the debate is truncated, leaving aside one of the debate's central themes, whether it is reasonable to believe that God exists. Even with that deliberate omission, there is much to talk about.

1. The Ills of Religion: An Inventory

Critics of religion often argue that its various evil consequences are interrelated. Religion must be authoritarian, for example, in order to sustain bizarre beliefs. So repression and the promotion of stupidity are part of a single package. Nevertheless, it is useful to tease out the various components of the New Atheist critique. Here is a brief review.

Religion promotes violence. Faith, charges Onfray, is responsible for "millions of dead in the name of God, millions on every continent and in every century" (2007, 182). Hitchens offers the reader a summary of "religiously inspired cruelty" he has witnessed in "Belfast, Beirut, Bombay, Belgrade, Bethlehem, and Baghdad" (2007, 18). Sam Harris asserts that "religion has been the explicit cause of literally millions of deaths in the last ten years" (2004, 26); indeed, religion for Harris is "the most prolific source of violence in our history" (27).

Religion divides humanity. Closely related to this is a second ill effect: religion's "wanton and carefully nurtured divisiveness" (Dawkins 2006, 262). Religions, and their respective adherents, are "*intrinsically* hostile to one another" (Harris 2004, 225). This divisiveness amplifies religion's propensity to encourage violence. As Harris puts it, "Faith inspires violence in at least two ways. First, people often kill other human beings because they believe that the creator of the universe wants them to do it. Islamist terrorism is a recent example of this sort of behavior. Second, far greater numbers of people fall into conflict with one another because they define their moral community on the basis of their religious affiliation" (2006, 80).

Religion is meddlesome and power hungry. Religion, claims Hitchens, "*must* seek to interfere with the lives of nonbelievers, or heretics, or adherents of other faiths. It may speak about the bliss of the next world, but it wants power in this one" (2007, 17). Christianity, agrees Onfray, seeks to control "the smallest details of daily life" (2007, 42).

Religion supports tyranny. Gods are always enlisted to "justify. secular power," notes Onfray (2007, 23). This is true no matter how odious the power in question: Christian leaders either actively supported the Nazis, or at the very least kept silent as Hitler bent Christianity's long-standing anti-Semitism to his own purposes.

Religion promotes stupidity. Religion "wholly misrepresents the origins of man and the cosmos" (Hitchens 2007, 4). As a result, charges Harris, America is becoming a "lumbering, bellicose, dim-witted giant." More than half of Americans, he claims, "believe that the entire cosmos was created six thousand years ago" (2006, x–xi). Because such absurdity cannot survive critical thought, "monotheism loathes intelligence" (Onfray 2007, 67). Faith, charges Dawkins, "is an evil precisely because it requires no justification and brooks no argument" (2006, 308).[1] Among other costs, religiously grounded stupidity leads to a deadly opposition to much of modern medicine (Hitchens 2007, 44–5; Harris 2006, 26). Apart from leading people to believe things that are obviously false, religion promotes beliefs for which there is no evidence, "propositions for which no evidence is even *conceivable*" (Harris 2004, 23). Thus, "to believe in a god is one way to express a *willingness* to believe in anything" (Hitchens 2007, 185).

Religion causes psychic deformation. All these ills are related to religion's impact on the psyche. Religion *arises* from psychic weaknesses, "from fear, misgiving, unease, inability to look death in the face, the feeling that something is lacking, and distress at the realization that human life is finite" (Onfray 2007, 35). It also magnifies psychic weakness, giving rise to various deformations. The believer must abandon "self-respect in order that one may squirm continually in an awareness of one's own sin" (Hitchens 2007, 7). Faith, suggests Dawkins, is "arguably a form of mental torture" (2006, 286). If the effects of this torture were confined to the believers themselves, they might be tolerable. But they are not: the "death instinct" at the heart of religion is regularly turned outwards, encouraging "contempt, wickedness, the forms of intolerance that produce racism, xenophobia, colonialism, wars, social injustice" (Onfray 2007, 67).

2. The Defenders Respond

The defenders offer various quick and easy answers to all these charges. How well do those answers hold up under scrutiny?

Those who "pass" vs. those who "flunk." In his debate with Hitchens, Douglas Wilson offers an intriguing response: the New Atheists are like someone who judges a professor, not by evaluating his attentive students alone, but also on the basis of "the dope-smoking slacker that he kicked out of class in the second week." That is, the New Atheists don't judge Christianity by looking at "those who believe the gospel in truth and live accordingly," but also on the basis of baptized Christians who treat its doctrines with contempt. "You are saying," Wilson complains, "that those who excel in the course and those who flunk out of it are all the same" (Hitchens and Wilson 2008, 28).

The New Atheists have an answer ready: the most dangerous believers are not those who have "flunked," they are those who have best learned the lesson. In this view, it is the most tolerant and reasonable Christians who are ignoring the prof. They are less obnoxious precisely because of their "unacknowledged neglect of the letter of the divine law" (Harris 2004, 18).

This type of claim is important enough to warrant serious attention, and I will return to it in chapter 4. For the time being, we should note that Wilson's argument, and the New Atheist response, immediately point to a key issue: just what is the "course" in question? What is the "true" religious teaching that someone or other has failed to absorb? This leads us to a second common response to the New Atheists.

Misrepresentation. Various defenders argue that the New Atheists' picture of religion is grossly distorted. Believers reading Dawkins, say the McGraths, "will simply find themselves appalled by the flagrant misrepresentation of their beliefs and lifestyles." Dawkins presents "the pathological as if it were normal, the fringe as if it were the center, crackpots as if they were mainstream" (2007, 13, 22). Haught extends the charge to the New Atheists as a whole: "Serving up the most extreme forms of rabid religiosity, they try to convince their readers that this repugnant material is the essence of faith" (2008, 28). For Edward Feser, the New Atheist image of religion is based on "absurd caricatures" (2008, 23).

The New Atheists can respond that the "fringe" is in fact the mainstream of Christianity, at least in America. As Sam Harris argues, "53 percent of Americans think that the universe is less than 10,000 years old ... and yet, religious moderates like Hedges invariably accuse me of 'caricaturing' Christianity whenever I criticize these beliefs" (2007).

Harris's response, however, is purely quantitative. Some of the defenders suggest that one must use a qualitative lens, and focus on faith as articulated by "the best representatives of religious thought" (Feser 2008, 87). Michael Novak urges us to "consider contemporary religious experience in the light of some of its most sophisticated and heroic practitioners" (2008, 32), and Keith Ward holds that we must "pay more attention to the sane, intelligent and

morally committed members of major religious communities"
(2007, 125).

The response obviously rests on some sense of what a "true"
representation would look like, or what the "best" variant of religion might be. If one reads this or that defender, one will come
across depictions of the true nature of belief. Keith Ward, for example, claims that "religion has often been a voice of moderation
and reconciliation, and *that is its true role*, as the scriptural documents of all the great world religions *clearly* state" (2007, 81;
emphases added).

Some readers may find such claims plausible.[2] But what happens if one reads a wide range of defenders? Then the face of "true"
religion begins to blur, becoming frankly contradictory. Consider,
for a start, the tensions between the "mainstream" and fundamentalist defenders. Liberal theologian John Haught comments that
his book is a critique both of the New Atheism and of the fundamentalist religion "against which it is reacting" (2008, xv).
Fundamentalist preacher Albert Mohler responds in kind: "The
New Atheism is new in its refusal to tolerate moderate and liberal
forms of belief. Now this [is] something that is genuinely helpful"
(2008, 60). The more conservative defenders seem particularly bit-
ter towards liberal Christians. Beale jeers at the "circus formerly
known as the Episcopalian church," and considers it "entirely possible" that the Archbishop of Canterbury is an atheist (2008, 13–14).
After rejecting the New Atheist claim that religion is mere wishful
thinking, Feser feels compelled to add: "I readily concede that
theological liberalism, like liberalism generally, *is* (in this respect as
in so many others) based on little more than wishful thinking"
(2008, 272). Eagleton reverses the relation: "The fundamentalist is
like the kind of neurotic who can't trust that he is loved, but in infantile spirit demands some irrefragable proof of the fact. He is not
really a believer at all. Fundamentalists are faithless" (2009, 114).

Given the sharp differences among them, it is not surprising that
the defenders' work as a whole offers no clear guidance on where
to find the "best" Christian thought, the thought that the New
Atheists have allegedly ignored. For Haught, Protestant theologian Paul Tillich is an essential reference. To ignore thinkers such

as Tillich, he declares, "is like trying to explain the natural world while leaving out any mention of modern science" (2008, 44). Hedges also relies on Tillich for an account of the true nature of faith (2007). Mohler, on the other hand, dismisses Tillich as an atheist (2008, 104)!

The defenders are similarly divided on a range of vital questions. Keith Ward embraces religious pluralism: "Those who hold religion back are those who stick to the view that only their religion provides a set of absolutely certain, unquestionable, definitive and unchanging truths, while everybody's else's religion is false" (2007, 198–9). Catholic theologian Thomas Crean takes a different view: "Nor need a Catholic be disconcerted by the great variety of religions in the world. We hold that God made man to know and love Him, but that this pure impulse, implanted in the human race at its creation, is resisted by many strong forces within and around us, which may wholly check it or turn it from its proper end" (2007, 158). If not for the "strong forces" that resist the "pure impulse" within us, everyone in the world would presumably be a good Catholic.

Apart from these tensions between the more liberal and more conservative defenders, the conservatives differ among themselves on vital matters. Rejecting the New Atheist claim that faith demands the suspension of critical thought, Dinesh D'Souza declares that "doubt is the proper habit of mind for the religious believer" (2007, 195). This is hardly the conclusion one would take from Crean. A person not raised a Catholic, Crean writes, may reason their way to the conclusion that "the Church is from God, and so her teaching is worthy of belief." But "from the moment that he possesses this light, it becomes wrong for him to begin again to question the truth of the Church's teaching, since that would be tantamount to doubting the veracity of God. The rational justification of the Catholic faith was a ladder by which he climbed to the point where he could receive the internal gift of faith. Having once received this gift, he has no more need of the ladder for himself, though he can still make it available for others" (2007, 148).[3]

Finally, we find sharp differences among the defenders on specific questions such as evolution or gay rights. On the latter question,

David Myers presents a "conservative, marriage-supporting posi-tive argument: that the world would be a happier and healthier place if, *for all people*, sex, love, and marriage routinely went to-gether" (2008, 78). For Edward Feser, such an idea heralds the end of civilized life: "If 'same-sex marriage' is not contrary to nature, then nothing is; and if nothing is contrary to nature, then ... there can be no grounds whatsoever for moral judgment" (2008, 150).

In summary: it is not entirely fair for Christian defenders to ac-cuse the New Atheists of painting a "false" picture of their faith, since even the defenders themselves present sharply divergent "true" pictures. On the other hand, those divergences, when com-pared to the generally monolithic image of Christianity found in the New Atheist works, do suggest that the latter are guilty of ig-noring the diversity of viewpoints within Christianity. And as we will see in chapter 4, on the occasions that they do mention that diversity, the New Atheists conveniently order Christian view-points on a spectrum from wishy-washy to serious, so as to save the argument that the "true" believers are the most dangerous.

Someone else's religion. Religious diversity supplies another easy strategy for dismissing the New Atheist critique: simply claim that the New Atheists are really talking about *someone else's* religion. Thomas Crean, for example, confidently declares that "some reli-gions, though not my own, teach or foster immoral doctrines" (2007, 118). Depending on which defender you read, the problem-atic religions are Islam, Christian fundamentalism, or both. The New Atheist understanding of Christianity, complains Haught, is based on "creationist and intelligent design theists" (2008, xi). After reviewing Harris's list of examples of recent conflicts inspired by religion, Beale comments that "nearly every example given here includes Muslims ... It is not the Jains, Mormons, Hindus, or Christians who are actively stirring up violence" (2008, 84). D'Souza agrees: "In the Muslim world, violence in the name of religion is still a serious problem. But for Christians the tragedy of violence in the name of religion is thankfully in the ancient past" (2007, 210).

But it is too simple to claim that wild-eyed Jihadists and corrupt televangelists are responsible for all that ails religion. The German clergy who managed to make their peace with Nazism were neither fundamentalists nor Muslims. Nor were the Chilean bishops who thanked Pinochet for responding to a "wish of the majority" by overthrowing a democratically elected government (Comité Permanente del Episcopado 1975), or the Argentine bishops who accepted the naming of Mary, the mother of Jesus, as an honorary "captain-general" of the armed forces during the murderous Argentinian dictatorship (Hebblethwaite 1982).

The New Atheists also deploy an interesting argument to counter the "someone else's religion" response: whether they like it or not, believers are in solidarity with one another. *All* believers provide "a cloak of respectability" to extreme belief, claims Dennett (2006, 299). Dawkins agrees that "sensible" religion is "making the world safe for fundamentalism by teaching children, from their earliest years, that unquestioning faith is a virtue" (2006, 286). And for Harris, "Religious moderates are, in large part, responsible for the religious conflict in our world, because their beliefs provide the context in which scriptural literalism and religious violence can never be adequately opposed" (2004, 45).

Some reject this argument out of hand: "No individual can possibly be held responsible for the actions of another individual over whom he has no authority or influence and has never even met," argues Beale (2008, 119). This legalistic defence is unsatisfying. Many people recognize that "enabling" is a morally dubious activity. The lawmaker who consistently fights against all forms of gun control because of donations from lobbyists is not *legally* responsible for gun crime, but many would recognize a *moral* culpability there. The key question is thus one of fact: do "moderate" believers in fact enable, providing "a cloak" for extreme belief? Serious consideration of this question would require a book in itself. We can note for now that the New Atheists' argument entails that we'd be better off without "moderate" religion.

A good thing for good people. Let us now turn to a last quick response to the New Atheist critique. When religion seems to lead to evil, the fault lies not with religion itself, but with people, religion's "human vehicles" (Myers 2008, 10). As Hedges puts it, religion is "a good thing for good people and a bad thing for bad people" (2008, 4).[4] The claim is puzzling in one respect: it makes it sound as if religion, which one might expect to *transform* people, is but a passive tool in the hands of good people or bad ones, as the case may be. Further, in viewing religion in this way, the claim echoes the "guns don't kill people, people kill people" argument.

And just what is the problem with the latter? Yes, guns generally don't fire unless someone pulls the trigger. Yet guns are designed for a narrow purpose: to do or threaten harm. They thus make it easier for an already violent person to hurt another. They can even encourage deadly violence, by making it too easy to pass from a violent desire to action. And they often hurt and kill unintentionally. Guns may require people in order to kill, yet they are clearly dangerous, even if one does not view them as "intrinsically" evil.

And religion? Could it also be profoundly dangerous, even if not "intrinsically" evil? Consider, for example, the New Atheist claim that religion divides humanity. If true, is this divisiveness purely a reflection of human weakness, or is it somehow built into religion itself? Keith Parsons suggests that "it is plausible that theism, with its insistence upon the existence of a single, all-important deity who demands the exclusive devotion of his followers, has a natural and spontaneous tendency to develop into intolerant and exclusionist forms" (2008, 55). Can an honest believer deny this *possibility*?

The gun analogy was suggested by the defenders' argument that, to paraphrase, "Religion doesn't hurt people, people hurt people." But one need not accept the analogy. Guns are deliberately designed to do or threaten violence. The believer need not accept that religion serves such narrow and negative ends. A critical believer might prefer the metaphor of *fire*, which is certainly dangerous, yet which also sustains life. If religion is fire, it is irresponsible to deny its intrinsic dangers. On the contrary, we must sharpen our awareness of those dangers and consider how best to mitigate them, without quenching the fire itself.

3. Conclusion

In this initial overview of the New Atheist debate, we first examined the range of charges against religion which, it is said, foments violence, divides people, props up tyrannical governments, meddles in people's lives, and tends to make its followers stupid and neurotic. While there are serious answers to these charges, the chapter limited itself to a critique of some of the "quick and easy" ones. We saw in particular that one of the most popular answers, that the New Atheists grossly misrepresent religion, stumbles on the inconvenient fact that the New Atheist portrait does resemble the outlook of many contemporary believers. Nor will it do to turn away from this merely quantitative fact and appeal to the "best" or "most serious" conception of religion, since the defenders are sharply divided on just which conception that might be.

We now move to a question that requires more lengthy consideration: the relation of religion to evil in history.

chapter two

Faith, Reason, Radical Evil

All participants in the New Atheist debate agree that, in some un-defined past, religious belief was the norm. In such a world, it would be natural to use religious language to justify any action, even to oneself. Recourse to religious language to rationalize ac-tion can be quite conscious and cynical. But not always: we are not necessarily clear on our own underlying motivations, and to un-derstand those motivations we turn to the explanations that are *available*. Philosopher Alasdair MacIntyre argues that "how indi-viduals understand their relationship to their own actions and how those actions are generated is in part a matter of the size and subtlety of the vocabulary available to them" (1988, 183). In a world saturated with religion, much of the vocabulary of self-interpretation would be religiously based.

In such a world both good and evil would be justified and un-derstood through religious language. The New Atheists display, however, a curious asymmetry in this regard: they regularly sug-gest that the historical evils of religion really are due to religion, while the good stuff is purely incidental.[1] Some have argued, how-ever, that many historical evils associated with religion are *also* in-cidental to it. William James gave a famous statement of this view, so this chapter will begin with his claim that religion is a mere pretext for evil done in its name. If this is true, then we would ex-pect to find as much violence and hatred in irreligious times as we do in religious ones. The defenders hold that the history of twentieth-century totalitarianism demonstrates this, and more.

But the New Atheists have a counter-argument: Nazism was either a Christian phenomenon, or at least one built upon Christian foundations. Other totalitarian states were also religious, in one way or another.

This chapter will consider these competing claims. We will take up the complicated relation of Christianity and Nazism. When we consider other cases of totalitarianism, we will see that the New Atheists' very definition of religion becomes slippery. Harris, in particular, shifts his target: the problem is no longer just religious belief, but any willingness to believe things without "evidence." We will challenge his confident belief that reason and a "taste for evidence" will deliver us from evil.

1. Mask or "Inner Force"?

Writing in 1902, philosopher William James offered an influential response to the charge that religion promotes hatred and violence. When we closely examine "the baiting of Jews, the hunting of Albigenses and Waldenses, the stoning of Quakers and ducking of Methodists, the murdering of Mormons and the massacring of Armenians," James argues, we find that "piety is the mask, the inner force is tribal instinct ... At most we may blame piety for not availing to check our natural passions, and sometimes for supplying them with hypocritical pretexts" (rpt. 1999, 370).[2]

The argument is a venerable one. Countering the argument that the abolition of Christianity would overcome divisions between groups, Jonathan Swift asked: "Are party and faction rooted in men's hearts no deeper than phrases borrowed from religion, or founded upon no firmer principles? ... Because religion was nearest at hand to furnish a few convenient phrases, is our invention so barren we can find no other?" (rpt. 1985).[3] Is the argument correct? Does religious piety merely "mask" the true motives of violence? The question is vital: if a mask is stripped away, we can expect that whatever motive is hidden underneath will soon supply itself with another mask. But if religion is a true cause of violence, then we could hope that a decline in faith would yield a reduction in barbarism. The twentieth century has offered us various experiments in post-religious life. The record is not encouraging. I do not wish to argue that we "cannot be good without God." The record suggests, though, that we are quite capable of being radically evil without belief in God. Indeed, the actions of Stalin, Mao, Hitler, and the Khmer Rouge lead one to wonder at Harris's claim that religion is "the most prolific source of violence in our history" (2004, 27). Unless, that is, twentieth-century totalitarianism was in fact a religious phenomenon. Let us consider this question.

2. The Contested Testimony of Totalitarianism

For the New Atheist, "there is no finer pleasure than recounting the history of religious brutality and persecution," comments David Berlinski, but "there is this awkward fact: The twentieth century was not an age of faith, and it was awful. Lenin, Stalin, Hitler, Mao, and Pol Pot will never be counted among the religious leaders of mankind" (2008, 19).

The New Atheists offer a different reading of twentieth-century totalitarianism.[4] For their purposes, the case of Hitler and Nazism is the most promising. Dawkins comments that Hitler "never formally renounced his Catholicism," and believed in "divine providence" (2006, 273).[5] Onfray also claims that Hitler "consistently and unambiguously expressed his admiration for Christianity," something which he claims to have learned from Hitler's "published conversations with Albert Speer" (2007, 187).[6] Both authors recognize that people can profess belief for quite cynical reasons (Dawkins 2006, 19; Onfray 2007, 143). So why are Hitler's public professions of faith taken at face value?[7] In a discussion of Hitler's *private* views, Martyn Housden cites his statement that he was dedicated to "eradicating Christianity from Germany root and branch. You are either a Christian or a German. You can't be both" (1997, 46).

Unlike Dawkins and Onfray, Harris and Hitchens don't paint Hitler as a Christian. Hitchens describes Nazism a "quasi-pagan phenomenon which in the long run sought to replace Christianity with pseudo-Nordic blood rites and sinister race myths" (2007, 237). Harris concurs: Nazism was an "explicitly anti-Christian movement" (2004, 100). But he also holds that "knowingly or not, the Nazis were agents of religion." Why? Because anti-Semitism was the child of "Christian theology" (79).

Christian writers such as German theologian Hans Küng have recognized that the Nazi persecution of the Jews would have been impossible without the long history of Christian anti-Semitism (1977, 169). But were German Christians so pathologically spiteful as to embrace Nazism for its anti-Semitism, and ignore the threat that it posed to Christianity itself? Many Christians saw the danger very clearly, and were disgusted as well by Hitler's race theories. But that clarity did not lead to a unified and sustained Christian opposition to the Nazis.

Before Hitler's taking power in 1933, the Catholic church in Germany seemed clearly to grasp the dangers of Nazism. Theodore Abel's fascinating collection of Nazi party members' written statements on their experience before 1933 cites a Nazi's recollection: "The church made life difficult for us ... We were barred from the sacraments, because we refused to leave the Party" (1965, 97). But at the end of March 1933, just weeks after parliamentary elections marked by widespread intimidation had given the Nazis 44 per cent of the national vote (Bullock 1962, 265),[8] the German bishops announced the "reconciliation of their church with the Nazi movement" (Times of London 1933a). And in July 1933, the Vatican signed a concordat with the Nazi government, "destined to render impossible any future conflicts between the Church and State in Germany," in the words of Vice-Chancellor von Papen (qtd. in Cortesi 1933). The agreement, the *New York Times* reported, "binds the German clergy against taking part in politics in any way" (ibid.).

What had happened? The shift in the church's official reasons is revealing. The pre-1933 condemnations referred to Nazi *doctrines*. The crucial declaration, one with which "the entire episcopate had eventually come into line" (Wolf 2010, 155), was issued in 1930 by the bishop of Mainz, who

declared Catholicism and National Socialism to be incompatible "because the program of the NSDAP contains precepts that are irreconcilable with Catholic doctrine and principles." These included the "overesti-mation of the Germanic race and the denigration of all foreign races ... that in many lead to complete hatred of foreign races," tendencies that were denounced as "unchristian and un-Catholic." (Wolf 2010, 141; elision in Wolf)

The bishop therefore "instructed the clergy of his diocese that no Catholic may join the Nazis, that Nazis may not attend Catholic funerals or other Catholic ceremonies, and that any Catholic who remains an inscribed member of the party may not receive the Sacrament" (Times of London 1930). But after the March 1933 elec-tions, official Catholic statements focus on church *interests*. The bishops' 30 March statement referred to Hitler's recent promise that church-state treaties would be respected and "the rights of the Churches would not be touched" (Times of London 1933a).[9] The concordat, for its part, declared that Catholics would now "enjoy all the rights and privileges hitherto possessed by the Protestants" and the Church was promised "complete freedom for the exercise of its spiritual mission" (Cortesi 1933).[10]

But it was highly problematic to divorce "political" and "spiri-tual" functions in a situation evolving towards totalitarianism, when any defence of human dignity and rights inevitably had a political dimension. The constraint accepted by the church thus weakened a source of resistance, an outcome celebrated by Hitler when he declared that the concordat ensured "that from now on German subjects of the Roman Catholic faith will unreservedly put themselves at the service of the new National-Socialist State" (Times of London 1933b). But was resistance still a live possibility in mid-1933? One observer later described the period as one when "there was still some faint glimmer of hope that [the Nazi] move-ment could take another and less disastrous course either through the disillusionment of its more moderate members or through ef-fective opposition from that section of the German people which opposed it." The observer was Pius XII himself (1945). Neither the bishops' "reconciliation" with the Nazis nor the concordat can be said to have encouraged that "faint glimmer of hope."[11]

Given that the Nazis failed to respect the religious guarantees of the concordat, and given the magnitude of the evil they unleashed upon the world, should the German bishops and the Vatican have accommodated themselves to the Nazi regime? Church officials did have legitimate reasons for fearing the marginalization of Catholic institutions, which would have made it easier for the Nazis to mobilize Christian religious symbolism as they wished, with little social counterweight. Still, it is hard to reject John Pawlikowski's observation that the church's outlook "so envisioned the Church and its purpose for existence that in moments of crises, where hard decisions were required concerning the institution's survival, non-Catholics occupied no central role in the definition" (qtd. in Hauerwas 2001, 346).

The Catholic Church was not the only one to come to terms with Hitler. Eberhard Bethge suggests that leaders in various churches initially saw Nazism as "an opportunity not to be missed," and believed that their acceptance of the Nazis would encourage "growth in the influence of the Church" (1970, 197, 204). And the churches were not alone in hoping to gain from Nazism. The vast range of those who invested hopes in Hitler is suggested in a 1933 *New York Times* review of *Mein Kampf*. After noting the book's appalling anti-Semitism, the reviewer commented: "Hitler is doing much for Germany, his unification of the Germans, his destruction of communism, his training of the young, his creation of a Spartan State animated by patriotism, his curbing of parliamentary government, so unsuited to the German character; his protection of the right of private property are all good" (Gerard 1933). The references to destroying communism, protecting private property, and curbing democracy are typical of the era: Hitler had targets other than the Jews, and many in the Western world approved of those targets. Historian Alan Bullock comments: "As the Army officers saw in Hitler the man who promised to restore Germany's military power, so the industrialists came to see in him the man who would defend their interests against the threat of Communism and the claims of the trade unions, giving a free hand to private enterprise and economic exploitation" (1962, 199). Among the factors explaining Britain's appeasement of Hitler prior to 1939, historian John Lukacs notes "the willingness of many Conservatives and at least a portion of the upper classes to give some credit to the then-new types of authoritarian governments in Europe, largely owing to their seemingly determined anti-Communism" (1999, 50).[12]

None of this is said to excuse Christians: They may not have caused the Holocaust, but they probably could have prevented it. In the Book of Proverbs, it is written: "Rescue those who are being taken away to death; hold back those who are stumbling to the slaughter. If you say, 'Behold, we did not know this,' does not he who weighs the heart perceive it? (Prov 24:11–12). Christians failed to rescue those being taken to death, and all-too-many later claimed "Behold, we did not know this."[13]

Our consideration of twentieth-century totalitarianism has touched only on the Nazis. The argument that religion bears a unique responsibility for violence in history must still deal with cases such as Stalin, Mao, and the Khmer Rouge. Dawkins and Onfray mention such cases only in passing. Hitchens and Harris, by contrast, tackle them directly, and they adopt similar strategies in doing so. For Hitchens, totalitarian regimes really are religious, whatever their rhetoric. Many saw Bolshevism as an "alternative religion" (2007, 244). North Korea is a religious state, marked by "debased yet refined" Confucianism (248). Even the Khmer Rouge has a religious dimension, since it "sought its authority in prehistoric temples and legends" (252). Similarly, Harris argues that the communism of Stalin and Mao was "little more than a political religion" (2004, 79).

One defender holds that this whole type of argument "should simply be laughed off as the shabby evasion it obviously is" (Hart 2009, 14). This will not do. The identification of religious features in some political phenomena is a practice of long standing. Tocqueville, who can hardly be dismissed as an anti-religious pamphleteer, argued that the anti-clerical French revolution "itself became a sort of new religion" (rpt. 1988b, 108). But we must distinguish two very different types of claims. The first recognizes that many political and social phenomena manifest "religion-like" features. The second holds that phenomena such as totalitarianism *really are* religions. Because the first claim, as we shall see, poses serious difficulties for the New Atheist argument, Hitchens and Harris gravitate towards the second.

Their argument is not a "shabby evasion," but it does lead to confusion. The problem is that we can no longer pin down what is meant by "religion." To turn atheist totalitarian regimes into religious ones, Hitchens follows a question-begging procedure, searching for characteristics of those regimes that, in his estimation at least, are also characteristics of existing religions. Having found qualities that he considers common to religion and totalitarianism, he can then declare the latter to be an instance of the former. This approach was critiqued long ago by, surprisingly enough, Marx and Engels. They noted the tendency of some "young Hegelians" to classify a wide range of phenomena as religious. As a result, "what religious consciousness and a religious conception really meant was determined variously as they went along" (rpt. 1976, 35).[14]

Like Hitchens, Harris defines religion as he goes along. He insists that "the actions of suicide bombers become completely unintelligible" without "the Muslim belief in martyrdom and jihad" (2004, 33). But Robert Pape, who studied every suicide bombing in the world over two decades, concludes that "the data show that there is little connection between suicide terrorism and Islamic fundamentalism, or any religion for that matter." In fact, Sri Lanka's Tamil Tigers, responsible up to that time for 40 per cent of all suicide bombings worldwide, were a Marxist organization "adamantly opposed to religion" (2003). How does Harris respond to this finding? Yes, he allows, the Tamil Tigers aren't really religious, but they "believe many improbable things" (2004, 229). As such, they are a quasi-religious group.

In Harris's approach, the defining quality of religion thus becomes its reliance upon "unjustified belief," its willingness to go beyond "evidence." And this, it seems, is the true evil: "the most monstrous crimes against humanity have invariably been inspired by unjustified belief" (2004, 79). The beliefs in question need not be explicitly religious. Rather, by virtue of being unjustified, Harris can treat them *as* religious. Humanity is now divided, not precisely between religious believers and non-believers, but between those who live by evidence and those who do not. Harris gives a very long and heterogeneous list of historical barbarities, including slavery, political executions, vivisection and child labour, and declares them to be the result of an "insufficient taste for evidence" (25). For Harris, it is the very failure to adhere to "evidence" that poisons religion itself. This failure turned "Jesus's principal message of loving one's neighbor and turning the other cheek into a doctrine of murder and rapine" because one becomes "capable of anything" once one believes in propositions without evidence (85).

We will examine various difficulties with Harris's strategy in a moment. But note that Hitchens and Harris have seriously blurred their argument. I suspect, for example, that Hitchens's book would have been met with more confusion than enthusiasm had it been subtitled: "How religions such as Christianity, Stalinism, and Nazism spoil everything." More importantly, the real or alleged similarities between twentieth-century totalitarianism and religions can be read in different ways. For the New Atheists, these phenomena demonstrate just how bad religion can be. But the same evidence could support the argument that, in the absence of religion, various underlying motivations will find another outlet. Perhaps many people feel a need to be "connected" to something "greater than themselves," or to be in contact with "the sublime."[15] If such a need exists, it could be met by religions, or by oppressive political movements decked out in pseudo-mystical clothing.

One may believe that the needs met by religion are an intrinsic part of human nature, in which case religion and humanity are made for each other.[16] Others may hold that the needs in question were created by religion itself. But a constructed need can still be a strongly felt need, as every advertiser knows. To the degree that religion has satisfied important needs, whatever their origin, it is hardly surprising that other human institutions should seek to emulate some of its features.

Sometimes this imitation is entirely conscious. Marx's most famous sentence about religion is that it is the opium of the masses. But he had something rather different to say about it late in his life. In 1881, Marx noted that "the dream that the end of the world was at hand inspired the early Christians in their struggle against the Roman Empire giving them confidence in victory." Marx went on to suggest that "scientific insight into the inevitable decomposition of the dominant order of society" plays an analogous role, being one of the factors offering a "sufficient guarantee" that socialism will triumph (1942, 387).

The sceptic might say that the "needs" that religion allegedly meets will wane over time should the world truly enter a post-religious era. But one cannot wave a magic wand and instantly abolish both religion and the needs associated with it. Even if the sceptic is right, we should expect a long transition period, in which certain unmet needs will be "available" for use and abuse. So the recurring manifestation of quasi-religious and pseudo-mystical traits in twentieth-century totalitarianism may point to an inevitable danger of any post-religion transitional period.

Some of the New Atheists seem aware of the danger, and recommend various nicotine patches to get us through the post-religious withdrawal. We must learn "to meet our emotional needs without embracing the preposterous" declares Harris (2006, 88). His particular solution, oddly enough, is found in Buddhist and Hindu "esoteric teachings" (2004, 283). These teachings are not religious and irrational, it seems, but rigorous and "empirical," a word that he stretches past the breaking point. For Harris, this tradition of Asian mysticism yields insights that are as far above anything available in Christianity as the physics of Cambridge is above the science of "the Bushmen of the Kalahari" (284).

Others stay on safer ground, seeking an emotional substitute for religion in science. Go read Stephen Hawking, Hitchens advises us, and "I shall be surprised if you can still go on gaping at Moses and his unimpressive 'burning bush'" (2007, 8). The exploration of the natural world, declares Dawkins, can "touch the nerve-endings of transcendent wonder that religion monopolized in past centuries" (2006, 12). Indeed, Dawkins sounds like an enthusiastic missionary to the "heathens" when he gets going on this topic: "My passion is increased when I think about how much the poor fundamentalists are *missing*. The truths of evolution, along with many other scientific truths, are so engrossingly fascinating and beautiful; how truly tragic to die having missed out on all that!" (283).

3. Reason to the Rescue?

Let us now examine Harris's claim that all sorts of evil spring from an "insufficient taste for evidence" (2004, 25). How precisely does a taste for evidence deliver us from evil? To form our beliefs only on the basis of evidence, to reject all "unjustified belief," is to declare our allegiance to reason. And reason, Harris confidently declares, "is nothing less than the guardian of love" (2004, 190). To embrace "reason," Harris feels, is to leave behind our "national, ethnic, or religious identity," and "learn to be mere human beings" (2004, 190).

But it is, first, dangerously dogmatic for anyone to think that all their important beliefs are grounded in evidence. However much one might hope that one's outlook on life is founded on a bedrock of unquestionable fact, life itself demands that we take some unproven beliefs for granted just to get through each day. Try to provide certain evidence that we should get out of bed on a Monday morning. Or that we are in love.[17] Or that something is worth fighting for. Or that life itself is worth living. We feel we have evidence to support these beliefs. But we make choices as to what will count as hard evidence in these matters, and what will not. Can we provide evidence to support our decisions on what is to count as evidence?

To Harris's warning that once we believe things without evidence, we become "capable of anything," we might answer that, *unless* we are willing to hold some beliefs without firm evidence, we are *capable of nothing*. We simply cannot live without commitments that may be fully reasonable, yet which go beyond firm "evidence": is your life worth living? Is it a good idea to marry your beloved? Should you care about future generations? If you really adopted Harris's dogma concerning "evidence," you would have to answer each of these questions: "Gee, I don't know." The natural endpoint of the rhetoric about evidence is not a brave freethinker. One must have reasons to be brave, to be free: these things don't come *naturally*. And those reasons will simply not be "scientific."

It is striking that Harris's *Moral Landscape* acknowledges the importance of commitments that cannot be justified by evidence, even for science itself: "Science and rationality generally are based on intuitions and concepts that cannot be reduced or justified" (2010, 204).[18] Despite this recognition, he retains the formula that condemns "faith itself – conviction without sufficient reason" (175).

But even if we cannot live entirely on the basis of beliefs for which we have evidence, we can presumably have a greater or lesser "taste for evidence." Unfortunately, this will not yield the great benefits that Harris supposes. It is naive to believe that reason must be the "guardian of love." Unfortunately, many forms of discrimination can appeal to reason and evidence. French feminist Simone de Beauvoir once commented that "when an individual (or a group of individuals) is kept in a situation of inferiority, the fact is that he *is* inferior. But the significance of the verb *to be* must be rightly understood here" (1961, xxiii). Oppress a people, and one will come to observe all sorts of pathologies. And those pathologies will provide ample evidence to justify the oppression.

The opponent of racism, sexism, or other forms of discrimination will argue that any systematic distinctions we observe between groups are themselves the result of the history of oppression. Undo the effects of that history, and we will see equality flourish.[19] But this is a claim that outstrips the evidence. Having been unable or unwilling to erase the effects of American slavery, for example, we cannot *know* just what might emerge from that erasure. But we can have *faith* in the proposition that we are created equal, that human talents are distributed randomly among groups, and that any systematic differences in talent we observe today are the results of inequality. This is a belief I myself hold, but it is an article of faith, not a certainty founded on firm evidence.

Even without a history of oppression, members of one group can find evidence for the inferiority of outsiders. We can easily judge members of another culture to be inferior, if we judge them according to our own cultural norms. We can look down on Saudis for their acquiescence to unfreedom, while they can hold us in contempt for our "decadence." In such judgments, we *are* relying on evidence, but we are uncritical about the standards with which we assess the evidence.

Perhaps *that* is the problem, not just an insufficient taste for evidence, but an insufficiently critical outlook. Perhaps we can save Harris's claim by tweaking it a little. Unfortunately, when we examine some of the great critical minds of human history, we are still unable to observe the power of human reason to tear down the barriers between us. Enlightenment, declares Immanuel Kant in 1784, is "man's emergence from his self-incurred immaturity." This immaturity is "the inability to use one's understanding without the guidance of another" (rpt. 1991, 54). What a glorious clarion call to modernity! But, Kant goes on, most people reject this freedom, through "laziness and cowardice." "It is so convenient to be immature," he sighs. In fact, the "entire fair sex" rejects "the step forward to maturity" (54). What's this? How does Kant *know* this? How can the philosopher famous for the critical lens he turned on human knowledge say such a thing? Why did his reason *fail* him on such an important question?

We turn to a sworn enemy of unjust authority, John Stuart Mill. His political philosophy is based upon one very simple principle: government is allowed to compel people *only* "to prevent harm to others." No one should force me to do something only because it is supposed to be in *my* best interest. "The only part of the conduct of any one, for which he is amenable to society, is that which concerns others. In the part which merely concerns himself, his independence is, of right, absolute. Over himself, over his own body and mind, the individual is sovereign" (rpt. 1974, 68).

Here is the cornerstone of our modern conception of individual freedom. But Mill is not finished: "It is, perhaps, hardly necessary to say that this doctrine is meant to apply only to human beings in the maturity of their faculties. We are not speaking of children … For the same reason, we may leave out of consideration those backward states of society in which the race itself may be considered as in its nonage" (1974, 69). "Nonage" means not yet of age, not yet mature. So entire *races* may be treated as children: "Despotism is a legitimate mode of government in dealing with barbarians, provided the end be their improvement" (69). One might have expected such a critical mind to stop at this point and ask: but are there *truly* peoples anywhere that are childlike? And how frequently do we find *evidence* in human history of despotism that has *truly* aimed at the "improvement" of its subjects? As with Kant, Mill's critical brilliance somehow failed him here.

Here, finally, is the great French thinker Alexis Tocqueville, dispassionate historian of the French revolution, brilliant observer of the young American democracy. Like Kant and Mill, Tocqueville wrote inspiring words about freedom. We must not seek it, he warned, merely as a means to material prosperity or other transient goals. We must cherish freedom for itself, cherish "the pleasure of being able to talk, act, breathe, without constraint." To seek in freedom a goal other than freedom itself, he warned, is to be "fit for servitude" (rpt. 1988b, 259). But here is Tocqueville writing in 1841 on the French invasion of Algeria. There are some, he notes, who "consider it bad that we burn harvests, that we empty the grain silos and that we seize unarmed men, women, and children." Tocqueville suffers from no such scruples: these are "regrettable" actions, he allows, but "necessities to which any people who would make war on the Arabs must submit." The right of war, he concludes, "authorizes us to ravage the country" (rpt. 1988a, 30, 78).[20]

With each of these three thinkers, we find the praise of modern freedom intimately linked with contempt for someone: for the lazy and cowardly, for the "entire fair sex," for those peoples not yet "of age," for those "fit for servitude," for "Arabs." In this respect, the children of the Enlightenment are not so different from the most arrogant of religious believers. There seems to be in human nature a deeply rooted desire for superiority and status. We will oppress others to gain superiority. Or we will look down on others to convince ourselves we are superior. "The most mediocre of males," comments de Beauvoir, "feels himself a demigod as compared with women" (1961, xxiv).[21] One's religion will serve nicely as a basis for such imagined superiority. But so too will one's race, one's sex, or even one's commitment to Enlightenment, to rationality, to *evidence*.

This quest for real or imagined superiority is so central to us that it shapes even our economic motives, which so many people today consider the fundamental root of human action. Adam Smith commented that "with the greater part of rich people, the chief enjoyment of riches consists in the parade of riches; which, in their eye, is never so complete as when they appear to possess those decisive marks of opulence which nobody can possess but themselves" (rpt. 1937, 172).

Reason alone will not save us from this deep-seated desire to assert our superiority, because reason itself is easily infected with it.[22] Speaking of philosophers, Rousseau commented drily that "each knows very well that his system is no more solid than that of the others, but he holds it because it is *his*" (rpt. 1966, 348). In his *Letter to a Christian Nation*, Harris comments: "Auschwitz, the Soviet gulags, and the killing fields of Cambodia are not examples of what happens to people when they become too reasonable" (2006, 42). This is correct, but "reason" and "reasonable" are not always close neighbours, except in the dictionary. In real life, even the most critical reason can be put to work in service of a profound unreasonableness.

4. Conclusion

The foregoing reflections are not intended to get religion "off the hook." Of themselves, they do not answer the question of whether religion is merely a mask for various forms of human evil, or a true cause of that evil. My guess is that the truth lies between those two endpoints. It is clear that people's readings of their sacred texts, and their overall understanding of their faith, are influenced by their life situation, by their milieux. A society riven by various types of contradictions, one that makes a mockery of people's hopes to live a reasonably happy life, can easily draw many to those preachers who focus on the most hateful elements of their scripture. This in turn can weaken the barriers to evil, even barriers rooted in their own religious tradition. Because of this, we must acknowledge that religion can help people commit great evil with an (apparently) clear conscience. Religion will never be a sufficient explanation of such cases: one still needs to understand the factors that led people to live their faith in a violent and hateful way. But religion can be an important *part* of the explanation.

Yet it remains true that evil does not require religion. It does not even require unreason. As we have seen, piety is not the only available mask for a will to dominate and denigrate: even "critical thinking" will serve quite nicely. And so, just as the believer is irresponsible to assume superiority over others, the "freethinker" also needs *consciously* to avoid this. Failure to guard against this temptation is damaging, not just to others, but to the very activity of thinking itself, because it allows thought to be made subject to the quest for superiority. Thought falls prey to a deep-seated instinct, one that wears different guises: the desire to edify one's "tribe" by denigrating some other tribe.

Unfortunately, many participants in the New Atheist debate repeatedly fall into this trap, as we will now see.

chapter three

Clashing Caricatures

To this point, we have generally focused on phenomena at a social level: religion, atheism. In this chapter, things get more personal, as we examine portraits of *believers* and *unbelievers* as individuals. Imagine, if you can, sitting down to read the works of the New Atheists at a single go. What picture would you gain of believers and unbelievers? Or what would one think of atheists, if one had met them only in the pages of the defenders? Take the first approach, or the second, or both, and you would likely come up with something close to the following composite sketches.

1. New Atheist Portraiture

Believers are *infantile*, in desperate need of delusions to get through the day: "Shh. Don't break the spell; these people need this crutch to keep their act together" (Dennett 2006, 134). "Men construct fables," Onfray says, "in order to avoid looking reality in the face" (2007, xvi). Believers, he asserts, accept "perpetual mental infantilism," because "they prefer the comforting fairy tales of children to the cruel hard facts of adults" (1). Hitchens writes of a school headmaster who told his charges that they will believe in God "one day, when you start to lose loved ones." That, Hitchens exclaims, "would be as much as saying that religion might not be true, but never mind that, since it can be relied upon for comfort. How contemptible" (2007, 4).

Given their need for "a metaphysical crutch in order to bear their lot" (Onfray 2007, 2), it is not surprising that believers are also *dogmatic*: "dyed-in-the-wool faith-heads," comments Dawkins, "are immune to argument, their resistance built up over years of childhood indoctrination" (2006, 5–6). Hitchens reports a sign outside an Indian preacher's headquarters: "Shoes and minds must be left at the gate" (2007, 196). Believers *can* be critical, Onfray allows, but only of other people's beliefs: "no one" is critical of their own (2007, 2).

Dogmatism is supported by the fact that believers are *not terribly bright*.[1] They are "often undereducated, informed only by the crumbs of information they are fed by the clergy" (Onfray 2007, 52). And this state of affairs is sustained by religious practice itself, "parrotlike repetition and the recycling of fables, with the help of well-oiled machinery that repeats but never innovates, which solicits not the intelligence but the memory. Chanting psalms, reciting, and repeating are not thinking. Nor is praying. Far from it" (52). The New Atheists do recognize the existence of theology, which would seem to challenge this picture, but does not. "Theological discussion and research," argues Dennett, is a ruse: it "scratches the skeptical itch" of a few and is "ignored by everybody else" (2006, 208).[2] And it's a dishonest intellectual exercise: "A millennium of theological sophistry, whole libraries of scholastic nitpicking have promoted the use of knowledge as a weapon designed less for honest argument than for apologia" (Onfray 2007, 53).

Believers are also *dishonest*. Dennett is certain that his book will face "ruthless misrepresentation when those who cannot honestly face its contents seek to poison the minds of readers to it or direct attention away from it" (2006, 412). "Sophisticated" believers, adds Dennett, are guilty of a particular form of dishonesty. They have left behind a primitive anthropomorphic understanding of the deity, yet they still call the object of their alleged belief "God," because they know that "brand loyalty is a feature so valuable that it would be foolish to tamper with it" (208). Dawkins echoes the charge: "Sophisticated theologians ... are happy to tell miracle stories to the unsophisticated in order to swell congregations" (2006, 59).

There are also many who are dishonest in professing belief for personal advantage. On at least five occasions in his book, Dawkins attacks the Templeton Prize, which he describes as "a very large sum of money given annually by the Templeton Foundation, usually to a scientist who is prepared to say something nice about religion" (2006, 19). He goes so far as to imply that there has never been a "really sincere recipient" (285). Others profess belief because they are afraid of persecution from true believers. In a word, they are *cowardly*.

Finally, believers are also *violent* and intolerant. On the basis of letters received after the publication of his first book, Sam Harris concludes that "many who claim to be transformed by Christ's love are deeply, even murderously, intolerant of criticism" (2006, vii).

The New Atheists do not limit their portraits to believers: they offer renderings of unbelievers as well. While believers are infantile, unbelievers are *mature and psychologically healthy*: "Atheism nearly always indicates a healthy independence of mind and, indeed, a healthy mind" (Dawkins 2006, 3). Atheism, declares Onfray, is "restored mental health," since unbelievers live beyond "magical thinking and fables" (2007, 4, 16). Unlike believers, unbelievers don't need to come together each week "to proclaim our rectitude or to grovel and wallow in our unworthiness" (Hitchens 2007, 6).

While believers are dogmatic, unbelievers are absolutely *open-minded*. Unlike believers, who "often bristle" when their beliefs are questioned, "atheists in general welcome the most intensive and objective examination of their views" (Dennett 2006, 16–17). In fact, atheists are *so* open-minded that, should believers show themselves to be in the right, Dennett promises that "we skeptics will not only concede this but enthusiastically join the cause" (17). They are, then, committed only to Truth, without petty attachments to their own particular views of the moment. As Hitchens puts it, he and his fellow unbelievers "may differ on many things, but what we respect is free inquiry, openmindedness, and the pursuit of ideas for their own sake" (2007, 5).

Unbelievers are generally *better educated* (Dawkins 2006, 102). As a result, they are also *more moral*, since "higher education, intelligence or reflectiveness" can "counteract criminal impulses" (229).[3]

Hitchens concurs: he is "sure" that a "proper statistical inquiry" would show that atheists commit fewer crimes of "greed or violence" than believers (2007, 5). Harris offers what he considers confirming evidence: "red" US states, those that vote Republican, have higher crime rates than "blue" states, and "it is no secret that the 'red states' are primarily red because of the overwhelming political influence of conservative Christians" (2006, 44–5). Even in the sphere of "family values," atheists come off better: atheists have the lowest divorce rates in the United States, while born-again Christians have the highest, according to Dennett (2006, 279).

While many self-declared believers are simply cowardly, atheists who publicly question religion are *courageous*. Dennett praises Harris's "brave" book, and decides to praise himself while he is at it: by questioning religion, he declares, "I risk getting poked in the nose or worse, and yet I persist" (2006, 299, 257). Onfray, for his part, is willing to run the risk of "character assassination" in his pursuit of truth (2007, 18).

In contrast to violent believers, unbelievers are, finally, *nonviolent*. As Dawkins puts it, "such hostility as I or other atheists occasionally voice towards religion is limited to words. I am not going to bomb anybody, behead them, stone them, burn them at the stake, crucify them, or fly planes into their skyscrapers" (2006, 281–2).

2. The Defenders Respond

It is harder to summarize the defenders' portrait of the New Atheists. Some of the responses to the New Atheist works are rather mellow: generally respectful in tone, they avoid name-calling and insult tossing. Myers is exemplary in this respect. With some exceptions, Novak also avoids caricature. But the less gentle responses to the New Atheists make up for the restraint of the others, leaving us with the following group portrait.

Atheists, first, are *degenerate*. Atheism, declares D'Souza, is the "Opiate of the Morally Corrupt": "If you want to live a degenerate life, God is your mortal enemy. He represents a lethal danger to your selfishness, greed, lechery, and hatred. It is in your interest to despise Him and do whatever you can to rid the universe of His presence" (2007, 261, 267). The reasoned arguments for atheism should thus not be taken at face-value: "When an atheist gives elaborate justifications for why God does not exist and why traditional morality is an illusion, he is very likely thinking of his sex organs" (269). Beale concurs, arguing that "many atheists become atheists during adolescence, an age that combines a tendency toward mindless rebellion as well as the onset of sexual desires that collide with religious strictures" (2008, 263).

Given that their posture is "mindless" and hormone-driven, atheists suffer from a profound *irrationality*, no matter how well educated they might be. The "irreligious worldview," declares Feser, is "deeply irrational, immoral and indeed insane" (2008, 5).

Atheists are also *social losers*. Atheists, claims Beale, "are one-third as likely to be married as the average American; these are the sort of men who believe that boring a woman with lengthy explanations of why her opinions are incorrect is the best way to win her heart" (2008, 17). If they do marry, he goes on, they are more than twice as likely to get divorced as Christians (188).

Having cast off God, the only source of true ethics, the atheist is also *morally adrift*. The atheist, says Ward, can "still believe in the importance of truth, beauty and friendship. Yet these seem to be purely personal preferences or hard-wired evolutionary survivals" (2007, 138). Crean concurs: "The atheist denies objective morality. He may say that he prefers to educate his children rather than to torture them, but he cannot say that he has a duty to do the one and to avoid the other" (2007, 156). "Logically," Crean goes on, "the atheist must be shameless, that is, inhuman" (157).

Some of the defenders go further: not only are atheists "logically" without moral ballast, they are also dangerously immoral in actual practice. Beale claims that only 89 "avowed atheists" have ever governed countries. Of these, 52 have "murdered at least 20,000 of their own citizens" (2008, 240). Beale thus endorses John Locke's "astute" position that atheists should not be "permitted to hold positions of political authority" (64). Berlinski, for his part, argues that "what Hitler did *not* believe and what Stalin did *not* believe and what Mao did *not* believe and what the SS did *not* believe and what the Gestapo did *not* believe and what the NKVD did *not* believe and what the commissars, functionaries, swaggering executioners, Nazi doctors, Communist Party theoreticians, intellectuals, Brown Shirts, Black Shirts, Gauleiters, and a thousand party hacks did *not* believe was that God was watching what they were doing" (2008, 26).

3. Caricature and Idealization

How do warring caricatures survive? Geographical or social distance will often do the trick: I can believe pretty much anything about people who live at the other end of the world, or who always move in social circles far distant from my own. That can account for the attitudes of many everyday believers and unbelievers, but cannot explain the views of the leading protagonists in the New Atheist debate, who are, presumably, personally familiar with individuals from the "enemy camp." How do their stereotypes survive such contact?

Social scientists have identified general mechanisms that sustain such beliefs, such as the tendency we all suffer to seek out information congenial to what we already believe. I wish to focus here on a particular mechanism that is glaringly obvious in many of the New Atheist debate's leading polemics: idealization. Imagine that you hear someone holding forth on the relative merits of atheists and believers. She seems to be talking about the way the people in her favoured group *are*, but in fact she is depicting the way she would *like* them to be. Consciously or not, this allows her to compare the others as (she thinks) they *are*, to her own *idealized* group.

Consider, for example, the New Atheists' depiction of the courageous "freethinker." The picture is based upon inference rather than observation: one *must* be brave to profess atheism since it can often entail personal costs. Professions of belief, then, can hardly be taken at face value, since they may simply reflect an unwillingness to pay the price of honest atheism. But this argument is undermined by other claims made by the New Atheists themselves. Dawkins asserts, for example, that top scientists today are generally atheists (2006, 100), and Hitchens comments that "belief among astronomers and physicists has become private and fairly rare" (2007, 70). If this is true, and if the contempt for the intelligence of believers manifested by the New Atheists represents a widespread attitude, then in many circles it would be a profession of belief, not of atheism, that requires courage. It is thus a question for sociological investigation which particular *milieux* are more supportive of belief and which of unbelief. While it would require rare courage for an American presidential candidate to proclaim himself a "freethinker," it might take some courage for an aspiring scientist to do the opposite.

And is the freethinker in fact a *free*-thinker? Is Dennett correct to claim that atheists are inherently open-minded, welcoming "the most intensive and objective examination of their views" (2006, 16)? A remarkably naive view is at work here: atheists have somehow transcended ideology itself. They are willing to put their views under the microscope because those ideas are no longer influenced by their social location, and no longer serve to rationalize their particular interests. As such, they would seem to have transcended the human condition itself.[4] The social sciences have taught us much about the interrelations among our existing beliefs, the information which we embrace or which we ignore, our life situation, our sense of our self-interests, and so on. Are atheists somehow exempt from this? If the New Atheists have evidence to this effect, it is a shame that they failed to include any of it in their work.

Moreover, to accept Dennett's claim, one would have to view the New Atheist books themselves as exemplars of open-minded fairness. This is not easy to do. Michael Novak comments that Dawkins, Dennett, and Harris "pretend that atheists 'question everything' and 'submit to relentless, almost tedious, self-criticism.' Yet in these books there is not a shred of evidence that their authors have ever had any doubts whatever about the rightness of their own atheism" (2008, 31).

Nor is it easy to detect open-minded fairness in the New Atheist treatment of specific issues. We noted Dennett's claim that atheists have the lowest divorce rates in the United States. Every

competent scholar knows what to do when faced with such a statistical claim: check it out, study the definitions and methodology
used in the study, see if other studies contradict the finding, and
check those out as well. Dennett manifestly failed to do any of this,
which suggests that when a "factoid" serves his purpose, fairness
falls by the wayside. Dennett's claim is based on a 1999 study by
the "Barna Group." It appears to be a very problematic study. Beale
claims that "Barna calculated divorces as a percentage of the entire
group, not as a percentage of marriages within that group." As
Christians are more likely than atheists to get married in the first
place, one can infer nothing about divorce *rates* from the study
(2008, 188). I cannot verify Beale's claim: the study is no longer
posted at the Barna website, which is another reason not to rely
on it. But the study's ambiguous title bears out Beale's claim:
"Christians Are More Likely to Experience Divorce than Are Non-
Christians," as opposed to "Married Christians ..." It is also telling
that Dennett cites the 2001 American Religious Identification
Survey (ARIS), but ignores that survey's divorce data, data that
suggest that Dennett's claims are exactly backwards (2006, 319).[5]
This is not the sort of modus operandi one expects from an open-
minded scholar.[6]

Before proceeding, we should guard against a misunderstanding. It is Dennett who unwisely chose to present divorce statistics
as evidence in a discussion of the morality of atheists and believers. In showing that Dennett's selective use of statistics undermines his claim to open-minded fairness, I don't wish to leave the
impression that I accept the underlying premise, that divorce rates
can be used as evidence of individual morality or immorality. Let
us imagine two couples: A is married to B, C to D. Both marriages
are marked by ongoing physical or emotional cruelty, inflicted by
A and C. B leaves the marriage, but D puts up with it, for a variety
of reasons. Are we prepared to assert that married D is more moral
than divorced B? This is surely a rash judgment. And we certainly
should not assert that divorced victim B is less moral than the married abuser C. I do not know what proportion of marriages end for
these reasons, but such cases undermine any simple link between
marital status and "moral fitness."

Idealizations that sustain dualist caricatures are not limited to one pole in the debate. Consider Dinesh D'Souza's response to the New Atheist claim that believers are dogmatic and unreasoning: "The believer embraces faith not 'blindly' but rather with his 'eyes wide open.' The Christian relies on faith not to suppress his native powers but to guide them so that they may see more clearly. He expects revelation to reactivate and guide his reason" (2007, 196). *The* Christian? Just what sort of claim is this? It is another idealization: the writer assumes that Christians, or perhaps "authentic" and "serious" Christians, are precisely what the author wants them to be.

Another Christian idealization is implicit, yet vital to the structure of the defenders' caricature of unbelievers: the failure to acknowledge just how *repellent* are the actions and omissions of many Christians. In his remarkable denunciation of atrocities committed by the European conquerors of the West Indies, sixteenth-century friar Bartolomé de las Casas tells the story of a Franciscan trying to convince a native chieftain about to be burnt alive that he should convert and so go to heaven. Are there Christians in heaven, asked the chieftain. Of course, the cleric answered. And so the chieftain, "with no hesitation, said that he did not wish to go there, but rather to hell, because he did not want to be in the same place as such cruel people." And this, added de las Casas, "is the fame and honor won for God and our faith by the Christians who have gone to the Indies" (rpt. 1813, 270).

But for many defenders, Christians play no part in the generation of atheism. Atheists arrive at their "irrational" world view as isolated individuals. "It may well be that if it weren't for that single commandment against adultery, Western man would still be Christian!" declares D'Souza (2007, 269). Beale likewise sees atheism as the product of the overheated hormones of the "morally corrupt." Could the defenders have hurled these casual slurs had they been willing to acknowledge the tremendous cost of sex scandals in various Christian churches? Many quite serious Catholics, in particular, have been deeply shaken by the widespread sexual exploitation of children among the clergy, and by church officials' enabling of that exploitation. While it may not be logically sound to jump from revulsion at such phenomena to agnosticism or atheism, neither is it terribly surprising.[7]

The defenders often fail to understand this key source of atheism, being in the grip of an idealized picture of believers. In turn, the New Atheists often cannot see just how crude are their portraits of believers and unbelievers, as they too are captured by idealizations.

4. The Geography of Belief and Unbelief

The clash of statistics put forth by the New Atheist debate's warring camps can lead us to miss some vital insights linked to the geography of belief and unbelief. Harris, as we saw, uses "red" and "blue" American states as proxies for belief and secularism. This produces findings that Dawkins endorses as "striking": where belief is strongest, crime rates are highest (2006, 229). Beale asks why Harris did not examine crime statistics by *county*, since they are reported at that level. Florida, notes Beale, is a red state, but its crime rates are highest in its blue counties (2008, 123). Harris claims that "Of the twenty-five most dangerous cities, 76 percent are in red states, 24 percent in blue states" (2006, 45). To which Beale replies: "twenty-one of the twenty-five most dangerous cities are located in blue counties" (2008, 124).

Just what is missed in this statistical duel? Social scientists often warn against the "ecological fallacy." This is committed when *aggregated* information is used to draw certain inferences about individuals. I observe, for example, that per capita sauerkraut consumption is higher in Germany than in Italy. Because the first country is traditionally Protestant, the second Catholic, I infer that "Protestants eat more sauerkraut than Catholics." You can see the mistake, of course. If we "zoom in" on the data, we might even find the relation reversed: perhaps German Catholics in fact eat more sauerkraut than German Protestants.

This is not statistical nitpicking. Both individual-level data and aggregate data can tell us something important about the effects of belief and unbelief, so long as we guard against errors of inference. Imagine a state in which conservative Christians wield substantial political power. They oppose, not just abortion, but sex education, the availability of contraception, and so on.[8] Those same Christians consistently urge their children to refrain from premarital sex, and isolate their children from at least some of the cultural influences that push in the opposite direction to abstinence.

We would expect to observe all sorts of contradictory phenomena in such a situation. At the *individual* level, it would not surprise us if rates of teen pregnancy, for example, were lower in conservative Christian families than in other families. Yet the state could also have much higher levels of teen pregnancy, even of abortion, than other jurisdictions, given its policies on sex education and contraception. It would be an error, the ecological fallacy, to infer from the state-level comparison that *individual* Christians had higher rates of teen pregnancy or abortions than other people. But it would be entirely legitimate to argue that the political clout of conservative Christians had a causal link to those phenomena at the aggregate level.

If one were then to "zoom in" from the state-level data to the level of counties, or even neighbourhoods or families, the political impact of the conservative Christians could disappear from view. One would be committing an error analogous to the ecological fallacy: looking for relationships at the wrong level. For insight into individual behaviour, one needs individual-level data. For insight into political effects, one needs data at whatever level those effects are likely to show up. If conservative influence is wielded at the state level, state-level comparisons will be most informative.[9]

Of the participants in the New Atheist debate, David Myers has offered the richest analysis of the puzzling statistics concerning the geography of belief and unbelief. Myers repeatedly finds stark contrasts between state- and individual-level relations. Thus, "the southern states have a strikingly higher rate of religious adherence and a slightly higher divorce rate." Yet those who attend religious services weekly are "half as likely to be divorced" as those who never attend services. Myers finds the same reversal for smoking and crime rates. Thus, in the United States at least, the more secular states "tend to be civil places." Yet "faith-active individuals are *less* likely to divorce, smoke, and be arrested" (2008, 66–71).

Myers suggests that the superior outcomes of more secular states in matters such as divorce or crime rates may be "thanks partly to their educated, higher-income populations" (2008, 71). This factor, though, can't explain the *international* differences in social outcomes. The United States has much higher rates of teenage births, sexually transmitted diseases, and abortion than the more secular nations of Western Europe (Berne and Huberman 1999). US incarceration rates are not only higher than those in other developed nations: they are the highest in the world (Walmsley 2008). At the international level, explanation in terms of "educated, higher-income populations" no longer holds: the United States is a world leader in both education and income, yet lags on many social indicators. So why do societies with a higher share of nonbelievers function better in many respects? Is this reality consistent with the claim made by many defenders that unbelievers are moral "parasites," living off (and squandering) the Christian West's religious inheritance? If so, why does that inheritance become more active and productive precisely as faith becomes less prevalent?

We cannot get at this question if we speak of belief and unbelief in the abstract. We must take account of how political power, religion, and culture have been intertwined in the modern Western world. The rise of the modern world was accompanied by a radical change in the mainstream Christian understanding of economic morality. Two important chroniclers of this change were sociologist Max Weber and historian R.H. Tawney. The two approached the issue from quite different angles,[10] yet were in broad agreement on the nature of the transformation that had taken place.

Both thinkers begin with a pre-modern period in which Christian institutions tried to temper economic acquisitiveness (though those same institutions were often implicated in that acquisitiveness). Of the moral doctrine of the medieval "Schoolmen," Tawney writes: "At every turn, there are limits, restrictions, warnings against allowing economic interests to interfere with serious affairs. It is right for a man to seek such wealth as is necessary for a

livelihood in his station. To seek more is not enterprise, but avarice, and avarice is a deadly sin. Trade is legitimate; the different
resources of different countries show that it was intended by
Providence. But it is a dangerous business" (1954, 34). Weber notes
that "quite considerable sums ... went at the death of rich people
to religious institutions as conscience money," which shows that
the rich themselves had doubts about the morality of their actions
(2003, 74).

The modern mood is clearly different. Though the Deuterocanonical book of Sirach declared, "As a stake is driven firmly into a
fissure between stones, so sin is wedged in between selling and
buying" (Sir 27:1–2),[11] Calvin could ask: "Whence do the mer-
chant's profits come, except from his own diligence and industry?"
(qtd. in Tawney 1954, 93). Examining the evolution of Christian
preaching over the period 1500–1700, Tawney notes the emerging
alignment between the virtues increasingly emphasized and "the
very qualities which economic success demanded – thrift, diligence,
sobriety, frugality" (1954, 97).

Over time, there is a shift in the hit parade of sins. Acquisitiveness
is but rarely condemned,[12] while Christian preaching becomes focused on matters such as sexual morality or alcohol consumption.
One hypothesis is that such a focus is "functional" for the new
economic order. Weber comments that the new emphases of religious doctrine supplied the employer "with sober, conscientious,
and unusually industrious workmen, who clung to their work as
to a life purpose willed by God" (2003, 177). But we must be cautious here: modern economic civilization is nothing if not flexible,
and can make good use of a wide range of behaviours. The "sober"
worker Weber associates with Calvinist preaching is good for
production. The "hedonistic" worker is good for sales.

Another explanation of the narrow focus on questions such as
sexual behaviour is that this is simply the morality "left over"
when concern for economic behaviour is removed from Christian
preaching. This sounds fanciful, but there may be an imperative
for the preacher to give listeners some specific things they can do
in order to enjoy some assurance of salvation. Weber argues that
the psychological need for such assurance triumphs over any

theological attempt to convince believers that they have no *right* to such confidence (2003, 110).

A final component of the emerging Christian doctrine is the view that helping the poor is morally problematic. While the long-standing Christian view was that a good deed done for the poor was done for Christ, charity comes to be seen as the encouragement of sloth. Hence, "the true Christian must repress mendicancy and insist on the virtues of industry and thrift," as Tawney summarizes the new outlook (1954, 98). Indeed, a forerunner of the implacable nineteenth-century political economists was the *Reverend* Joseph Townsend, who inveighed against laws that he found excessively generous to the poor. "Hunger will tame the fiercest animals," Townsend argued; "it will teach decency and civility, obedience and subjection, to the most brutish, the most obstinate, and the most perverse" (rpt. 1817, 23). Unfortunately, "our laws have said, they shall never hunger" (15).

While we may think of the Puritans as long gone, Tawney's depiction of the Puritan consciousness strikes a familiar chord: "Convinced that character is all and circumstances nothing, he sees in the poverty of those who fall by the way, not a misfortune to be pitied and relieved, but a moral failing to be condemned, and in riches, not an object of suspicion – though like other gifts they may be abused – but the blessing which rewards the triumph of energy and will" (1954, 191).[13] When Christianity takes *this* form, it should not surprise us that a "godly nation" is ill equipped to address poverty and inequality, and all the social ills associated with them.

Let us review the argument. Rather than dismiss the evidence that more secular regions and countries have been better able to address the social challenges of the modern world, we turned to history in order to explain the puzzles presented by the geography of belief and unbelief. A general lesson here is that we should be cautious in drawing direct inferences from religion in the abstract to various social outcomes, but consider the impact of particular religious forms, and their interaction with political and economic phenomena. At the same time, the evidence shows that it is quite illegitimate to equate the spread of secularism with moral chaos.

On the contrary, it is possible that secularism freed a humanitarian legacy of the Christian tradition from the domination of the more recent Christian currents.[14]

5. Conclusion

We have seen that both sides in the New Atheist debate indulge in caricatures. These are sustained by familiar mechanisms: social distance, for some people, confirmation bias, and idealization, on which we focused. The prevalence of idealization in the debate suggests some questions that might be asked of defenders and New Atheists, respectively.

Of the defenders, we can ask: is the religion you defend "actually existing religion," religion as it is in the world, with all its messy links to the full range of human needs and passions? If not, what is it exactly? Can you acknowledge that at least one of the spurs to atheism is the messiness of "actually existing religion"?

To the New Atheists, we may put various questions: Is the mature, intelligent, open-minded, morally superior, brave atheist you portray in your writings the product of an honest examination of "actually existing atheists"? Do not the very caricatures you present undermine your own claim to open-mindedness? And as to that, why do you believe that "freethinking" atheists are exempt from the effects of ideology? Are you not indulging in magical thinking here?

And of both parties in the debate, we should ask: When the New Atheists and the defenders talk about religion and atheism, about believers and unbelievers, *do you think they are talking about the same things*?

The leading voices of the New Atheist debate are unlikely to accept this chapter's critique of their dualism. A simple and comforting binary outlook might be sustained if one focuses, not on believers and atheists in general, but on the most "serious" among them. To this argument we now turn.

chapter four

The Serious and the Wishy-Washy

The nineteen suicide bombers of New York and Washington and Pennsylvania were beyond any doubt the most sincere believers on those planes.

Christopher Hitchens (2007, 32)

In the year 2006, a person can have sufficient intellectual and material resources to build a nuclear bomb and still believe that he will get seventy-two virgins in Paradise. Western secularists, liberals, and moderates have been very slow to understand this. The cause of their confusion is simple: they don't know what it is like to *really* believe in God.

Sam Harris (2006, 83)

Like the modern jihadists who strip away the moderate fiction of a religion of peace, Onfray does not hesitate to reveal the grinning skull of atheist post-nihilism that lurks beneath the obsequious smile of secular humanism.

Theodore Beale (2008, 199)

Sooner or later a generation may come along that takes the metaphysics of atheism with deadly seriousness. This was the fate of a highly cultivated nation in the Europe of our time, Germany, before it voted its way into Nazism.

Michael Novak (2008, 52)

There is a symmetry to these quotes. The New Atheist asserts that when believers get serious, they get ugly. The defender asserts that when atheists get serious, they get ugly. These claims are a vital support to the mutual demonization that characterizes the New Atheist debate. Each side can allow that there are decent members of the opposing camp, but then claim that the decent types are not fully serious, not true to their fundamental world view.

Yet there is also an important difference in the claims. The New Atheist says that, *as a matter of observable fact*, there is a link between serious belief and a thirst for violence. The defenders' claim is that, *as a matter of underlying logic*, there is a link between serious atheism and a dangerous, even genocidal, nihilism. We need to deal with these claims in different ways, because they are built upon different types of mistakes. The New Atheist claim is based on errors of fact and unexamined assumptions about human psychology. The defenders' claim, by contrast, reflects deeply held assumptions concerning how the whole set of legitimate human beliefs about right and wrong relates to belief in God. Chapters 6 and 7 will address those assumptions. This chapter critiques the New Atheist equation of serious belief with violence and intolerance.

1. The New Atheist Understanding of Serious Belief

To utter the phrase "beyond any doubt" is to reveal more about oneself than is perhaps wise. In this chapter's opening epigraph, Christopher Hitchens gives us a glimpse of what constitutes for him the limits of the thinkable. He simply can't conceive of the possibility that any of the innocent victims of September 11 might have held a deeper faith than that of their butchers.[1] Harris concurs: when a person "believes – *really* believes– that certain ideas can lead to eternal happiness," he must be intolerant. Harris cites Will Durant for support: "Tolerance grows only when faith loses certainty; certainty is murderous" (2004, 13).

So the "true" believer is possessed of a murderous certainty. This certainty is buttressed by a literal approach to scripture. Of Baruch Goldstein, who murdered twenty-nine Palestinians at Hebron in 1994, Hitchens observes: "An easy way to spot an inhumane killer was to notice that he was guided by a sincere and literal observance of the divine instruction" (2007, 208).[2] Literalism *must* lead to violence and intolerance, because of the nature of sacred scripture itself: "A literal reading of the Old Testament," claims Harris, "not only permits but *requires* heretics to be put to death" (2004, 82).

And what of the less-than-serious believers? Their reasonableness, such as it is, reflects "unacknowledged neglect of the letter of the divine law" (Harris 2004, 18). Moderates "pick and choose which parts of scripture to believe, which bits to write off as symbols or allegories," says Dawkins. There is no logic or rigour to this; it is a "matter of personal decision" (2006, 238). And so, religious moderates shake our heads in disbelief at the crimes of more committed believers, since our uncertain and timorous faith has robbed us of the capacity to grasp "what it is like to *really* believe in God" (Harris 2006, 83). An obvious implication is that the (relative) reasonableness of the moderates arises not from belief, but from disbelief, from having fallen away from pure belief in a compromise with modernity. So why not finish the process and abandon faith altogether? Why settle for half-sanity?

We can summarize the foregoing claims thus:

(a) Certain, serious belief requires a literal interpretation of scripture	(a) Uncertain, wishy-washy belief requires a non-literal interpretation of scripture
(b) And leads to violent intolerance	(b) And permits tolerance

2. Certainty and Violence

Let us first tackle the alleged relation between certainty and violent intolerance. Why exactly does someone require theological or ideological certainty before unleashing violence? We know that in many people violence requires little justification, theological or otherwise. Think, for example, of phenomena such as "road rage."

But that, one might answer, is everyday, trivial violence, while the violence of a suicide bomber is another thing altogether. That assumes what needs to be proved. Are we sure that such violence is not concocted, like everyday forms of latent or manifest rage, out of a thousand real or imagined grievances? Perhaps there is something horribly *banal* underlying the outbreaks of violence that have transfixed us since September 11. It might be said that such an argument is "relentlessly oblivious to what jihadists themselves say about their own motives" (Harris 2010, 155). "Given the clarity with which they articulate their core beliefs," Harris insists, "there is no mystery whatsoever as to why certain people behave as they do" (157). Harris's insistence is odd, given that earlier in the same book he attacks the "illusion" that "we are the authors of our own thoughts and actions" (103).

Indeed, when it comes to understanding heinous acts, relying on the perpetrators' explicit justifications is particularly unwise. Let us note two considerations that complicate matters. First, *uncertainty* may lead to violence. In their study of ethnic violence, James Fearon and David Laitin point to various cases (the Basques in Spain, Sikhs in India, Muslims in Kashmir) where violent ethnic movements were sparked by fears of assimilation into the mainstream (2000: 856–7). Fanaticism, as theologian Paul Tillich put it, "shows the anxiety which it was supposed to conquer, by attacking with disproportionate violence those who disagree and who demonstrate by their disagreement elements in the spiritual life of the fanatic which he must suppress in himself" (1952, 49).

Moreover, while the terror of 9/11 was linked to a particular understanding of Islam, this required that the terrorists be divorced from traditional Islamic teachings, that they be *freed of long-standing certainties* regarding right and wrong. As Bernard Lewis notes: "The callous destruction of thousands in the World Trade Center, including many who were not American, some of them Muslims from Muslim countries, has no justification in Islamic doctrine or law and no precedent in Islamic history" (2003, 154).

An interesting insight into the psychology of violence was provided during the Danish cartoon controversy of early 2006. As protests raged throughout the Islamic world, Amr Khaled, "the first contemporary Muslim televangelist" (Shapiro 2006), issued a "Message to the World." Those who took to the streets to protest the cartoons, Khaled declared, were upholding "the great Islamic concept of dignifying Allah's Messenger." In a striking passage,

Khaled depicts Muslims appearing before Muhammad on the Day of Judgment. They will say: "Perhaps we may have been wrongdoers, perhaps we sinned and perhaps we did not always work perfectly to reform and revive your ummah [nation] but we could not but dignify you and make the whole world dignify you." And Muhammad will answer: "Yes, you made mistakes and committed sins, but dignifying me was so dear to you." Hence, their mistakes and sins will be forgotten (2006).

Imagine a listener *uncertain* about his own status, his own standing in the eyes of God. Perhaps, suggests Khaled, he is a "drug user," or a "failure" in life. But vigorous protest in defence of his Prophet will wipe the slate clean. The psychological appeal of the image is unmistakable. Perhaps that is why discourses of mobilization often turn to it. Thucydides has Pericles argue in his famous "Funeral Oration" during the Peloponnesian War that the dead have "blotted out evil with good, and done more service to the commonwealth than they ever did harm in their private lives" (2.42). The deal offered by both Amr Khaled and Pericles also resembles the Catholic Church's offer of a "plenary indulgence" to those who took part in "wars against the infidels" (Hinojosa y Naveros 1908).

There is absolutely no need for the listener to be *certain* that Amr Khaled's understanding of Muhammad is correct. The listener may even think it highly improbable that Muhammad (or Allah, for that matter) will be particularly impressed by one's participation in burning down a Danish embassy. But that gesture is relatively costless, so why not give it a try, on the off-chance that Khaled is right?

But what of more costly gestures? What of the suicide bomber? Or, for that matter, what of the medieval Christian who took up the church's offer and joined the crusades? Surely they must believe firmly in the deal on offer? Not necessarily. Risking one's life is not always seen as a cost. Many people are suicidal, or just weary of life, or fearful of their future. Others may "prefer a short period of intense pleasure to a long one of mild enjoyment, a twelvemonth of noble life to many years of humdrum existence," as Aristotle put it (*Ethics*, 1169a). Others may value their lives, yet be so consumed with anger that they are willing to strike out, whatever the personal cost. Such intense anger needs no theological fuel.

Uncertainty can breed violence. But matters need not rest there. "Everyone seeks reasons for their passion," suggested Proust (1988a, 402). As beliefs can flow from actions as much as actions from beliefs, so can violence generate the certainty that justifies it. The insight is ancient: one biblical story tells of how Amnon raped his sister Tamar, after which he "hated her with very great hatred" (2 Sam 13:14–15).[3] So a rigid certainty, be it religious or otherwise, can be the product of violence, rather than its cause. I *will* enjoy the certainty that I am right, *because* I have committed crimes, and certainty is the only way I can justify myself in my own eyes.

The assumption underlying the New Atheist argument that "certainty is murderous" is that actions flow from beliefs. But beliefs can also flow from actions. Indeed, the influence runs in both directions. Consider Sartre's account of the young man he met in prison, who read his failure at everything he tried as a "sign that he was not made for secular triumphs," and hence joined the priesthood (1970, 48). Clearly, a metaphysical outlook gave him an interpretive key that others might find odd: his beliefs thus influenced his actions. But *what happened next*? He went to a seminary. And there he would have undergone training, a training that certainly shaped his subsequent beliefs: no seminary would consider the beliefs that brought someone to its door adequate for the mission they were to undertake after they left. So a certain milieu, with its set of beliefs and actions, led him to interpret his life in a certain way, leading him to a decisive action that reshaped his beliefs.

Consider now another "total" organization: a radical, clandestine group. Imagine an individual with some vague concern about *something*: salvation, perhaps, or the occupation of Palestine, or a lack of employment prospects. This concern leads to a tentative involvement, perhaps in some context only loosely related to the radical group, such as religious services led by a preacher who enjoys the trust of the clandestine movement. It doesn't take much in the way of clear beliefs to produce this first step, but much may happen in consequence. If the person seems "promising," they may be introduced to someone in a front organization. Eventually, they may be recruited into the clandestine group itself. But that group, like the seminary, will *never* accept the recruit's pre-existing set of beliefs as an adequate basis for radical action: there will always be ongoing indoctrination. Lawrence Wright's history of the September 11 attacks notes that it took some work to convince al Qaeda members to ignore the inconvenient fact that "the Quran explicitly states that Muslims shall not kill anyone, except as punishment for murder." In the early going, even close followers of al Zawahiri "were alarmed both by the death of innocents and by the use of suicide bombers" (2006, 124, 218). Murderous beliefs did not lead them *into* al Qaeda: al Qaeda led them to their beliefs.

So, yes, beliefs lead to actions. But if the action in question leads someone into a new milieu, it in turn will foster new beliefs. The "certainty" that eventually leads someone to blow up himself and others may be termed "theological" or "political," but it will almost always be *organizational* as well, the product of indoctrination under strictly controlled conditions.

3. "Acrobatic Avoidance" of Scripture?

We turn now to the New Atheist claim that a literal reading of scripture is a central marker of serious belief. Under the pressure of modernity, religious moderates have abandoned scriptural literalism, and gradually abandoned a set of beliefs "suggestive of mental illness" (Harris 2004, 72). Harris cites a grim passage from the book of Deuteronomy: should anyone, even your brother or child, try to lead you away from the true faith, "you shall kill him, your hand shall be first against him to put him to death" (Deut 13:9). He then infers that it requires "acrobatic avoidance" of such scriptural passages for us to "escape murdering one another outright for the glory of God" (2004, 78). The moderate's retreat from scriptural literalism is inspired, *not* by scripture itself, but by wider "cultural developments," the "hammer blows of modernity" (17). The direct result of this acrobatic avoidance, says Onfray, is that we are left with "a mere signifier, emptying it utterly of what it once signified. At which point we are worshipping an empty shell, prostrating ourselves before nothing – one of the many signs of the nihilism of our era" (2007, 209).

But a non-literal approach to scripture cannot be the product of modernity, because we find it throughout the entire history of Christianity. The refusal to embrace the literal reading of every last line of scripture does not constitute a wishy-washy capitulation to modernity: it represents the dominant approach to scripture throughout history. As such, there is no reason to view it as a half-way house to unbelief. After refuting the claim that Christians have traditionally read scripture literally, we will consider various fallback positions, variations on the claim of historical literalness.

What, first, do we mean by "literal"? The *Concise Oxford Dictionary* (Sykes 1976) defines "literal" as "taking words in their usual or primary sense." But then can *anyone* take all scripture literally? Consider the following biblical phrases gathered by one theologian:

Have you an arm like God, and can you thunder with a voice like his? (Job 40:9)

I saw the Lord sitting upon a throne. (Is 6:1)

The Lord ... stands to judge his people. (Is 3:13)

The eyes of the Lord are toward the righteous. (Ps 34:15)

Read literally, these all support the claim that "God is a body." Against that simple reading, the theologian opposes a single Gospel phrase, which he considers decisive:

God is spirit. (Jn 4:24)

The theologian in question, Thomas Aquinas (*Summa Theologica* 1, q. 3, a. 1), wrote more than eight hundred years ago: hardly a hapless victim of the "hammer blows of modernity."

But perhaps we can read scripture literally, so long as we are not too literal about what we mean by "literal." "The literal sense," declares Aquinas, "is that which the author intends ... When

Scripture speaks of God's arm, the literal sense is not that God has such a member, but only what is signified by this member, namely operative power" (*ST* 1, q. 1, a. 10). By our first definition of "literal," we might call this a "non-literal definition of literal."

Our original definition contrasted literal with figurative language. If we interpret "arm" as "arm," we interpret literally. If we interpret it as "God's power," we interpret figuratively, non-literally. With our second definition, the contrast changes: the 1943 papal encyclical *Divino Afflante Spiritu*, defining the task of the biblical interpreter, comments: "Just as he must search out and expound the *literal meaning* of the words, intended and expressed by the sacred writer, so also must he do likewise for the *spiritual sense*, provided it is clearly intended by God" (para. 26; emphases added). Literal is now contrasted with "spiritual." While the literal meaning is intended by the human author, a "spiritual sense" may find its way into scripture, behind the author's back, as it were. To find the literal meaning now requires interpretation, as the author's intention is not always explicitly stated. The encyclical observes that the literal meaning must be *searched out*, it is not immediately obvious. This understanding of literalness, then, will offer no comfort to the fundamentalist who holds the view that the truths of scripture are directly accessible, without need of human interpretation.

Does this position *work*? If we were to use the revised definition of "literal," would we be able to say that Christians have read the Bible literally, until the present day? No. In fact, not even the New Testament authors read the Old Testament literally, in *either* sense of literal, and they stand at the head of a whole tradition of biblical interpretation that neither understands words "in their usual or primary sense" nor restricts itself to the author's intended meaning.

New Testament writers indicated that many Old Testament passages were to be re-interpreted in the light of Christian beliefs. In Paul's letter to the Galatians, we read:

> For it is written that Abraham had two sons, one by a slave and one by a free woman. But the son of the slave was born according to the flesh, the son of the free woman through promise. Now this is an allegory: these

> women are two covenants. One is from Mount Sinai, bearing children for slavery; she is Hagar. Now Hagar is Mount Sinai in Arabia; she corresponds to the present Jerusalem, for she is in slavery with her children. But the Jerusalem above is free, and she is our mother. (Gal 4:22–6)

Of this passage, Northrop Frye comments: "A Jewish reader of Paul's interpretation, seeing that the Jews are identified with the Ishmaelites and the Christians with the Jews, might well say that this view of the story was about the most preposterous that it was possible to hold, and that a method of this kind could say anything about anything" (1991, 77). Jews most certainly did *not* identify themselves with the Ishmaelites, who were an alien people, sometimes depicted as hostile to Israel (Ps 83:6). Paul was not taking the words of Genesis in their "usual sense." Nor could one plausibly argue that he had discovered the "intended meaning" of the original Old Testament author.

The interpretive practices of the New Testament authors allowed later writers to engage in similar forms of interpretation. Thus, when Paul says of the rock from which water flowed in the Old Testament Exodus story, "the Rock was Christ" (1 Cor 10:1–4), Augustine seizes on the phrase, commenting: "The explanation of one thing is a key to the rest." Thus, the rock is Christ. But so too is the manna, "the living bread which came down from heaven." And so too are "the cloud and the pillar Christ, who by His uprightness and strength supports our feebleness." And finally, "In the clouds and the Red Sea there is the baptism consecrated by the blood of Christ" (rpt. 1887, 193). In short, as Augustine writes elsewhere, "The New Testament lies hidden in the Old" (qtd. in Brown 1968, para. 71.40).

Many Christian writers thought the same. Various Old Testament characters were said to "prefigure" Jesus. Job, because he was a just man like Jesus, argued Zeno of Verona in the fourth century (rpt. 1975, 222–3). Moses, because he "smote lawlessness and deprived injustice of its offspring" (Melito of Sardis rpt. 1999, 34). And in carrying the wood with which he will be sacrificed, Isaac is a figure of Christ (Origen rpt. 1982, 140–1). In the same way, Old

Testament events prefigured New Testament realities. For the fourth-century bishop Ambrose, "holy baptism was prefigured" by Israel's passage through the Red Sea in its escape from Egypt (rpt. 1896, 318).

So even a watered-down understanding of "literal" fails to capture traditional approaches to scripture: the New Testament authors and the Christian writers who followed them regularly went beyond the "intended meaning" when interpreting the Old Testament. Let us now consider another fallback position. Perhaps ancient writers took liberties with the Old Testament only, and read the New Testament literally. On the contrary, early Christian writers subjected both Testaments to a "spiritual" reading. In a sermon on the wedding at Cana, for example, fifth-century Bishop Faustus of Riez notes that the event took place "on the third day" (Jn 2:1). This is enough to establish that the wedding represents the joy that comes with the Resurrection. Jesus changes water into wine at Cana: "that is, the law gave way, grace succeeded: the shadow is removed, the truth is demonstrated" (Faustus of Riez rpt. 1975, 110). For Augustine, the Samaritan woman who meets Jesus at the well in the Gospel of John represents the Church, "not yet justified" (rpt. 1888a, 101). And Mary the mother of Jesus *also* stands in for the Church, according to the twelfth-century Abbot Isaac of Stella (rpt. 1975, 46).

These allegorical interpretations predate the Reformation. So yet another fallback position might be suggested: perhaps this tradition of interpretation is a specifically Catholic deviation, rejected by Reformation theologians. It is certainly true that the Reformers sought to rein in allegorical readings of scripture. Luther thus critiques Augustine, who resorts to "extraordinary trifling in his treatment of the six days [of creation], which he makes out to be mystical days of knowledge among the angels, not natural ones" (rpt. 1958, 4).

This argument, however, entirely undermines the New Atheist claim that believers have only moved away from a literal understanding of the Bible under the pressure of modernity. The latest fallback position holds the opposite: only when the Reformation appears on the scene at the dawn of the modern world does the literal reading of scripture gain ascendancy.

In any case, the position claims too much. If we hold to any recognizable definition of "literal," one cannot claim that non-literal readings of scripture disappear with the Reformation. Here is Luther, commenting on the book of Psalms:

> "Blessed is the man who walks not, etc." (Ps 1.1). *Literally* this means that the Lord Jesus made no concessions to the designs of the Jews and of the evil and adulterous age that existed in His time ... Ps 2:1 says: "Why do the nations conspire, etc." *Literally* this refers to the raging of the Jews and Gentiles against Christ during His suffering ... Ps 3:1 reads: "O Lord, how many are my foes." This is *literally* Christ's complaint concerning the Jews, His enemies. (rpt. 1974, 7; emphases added)

Such readings clearly fail to conform to either of the senses of "literal" discussed above. Words are not being read in their usual sense, nor can one plausibly argue that the intended meaning of the Jewish author of the Psalms was to condemn the Jews, as Luther repeatedly suggests. Luther's application of "literal" to interpretations that go well beyond the literal sense of the words in question suggests the following hypothesis: what is called a literal reading is often just a particular interpretation, one that is not acknowledged as such.[4]

Let us now consider another possible fallback position. "OK, fine," someone might say. "But none of what you have said touches on the central issue. For the Christian, the key question is not whether the Red Sea is a symbol of baptism, it's *what am I to do*? The Bible gives us many commands. And *those* are to be taken literally, and obeyed as the very word of God. Anything else, and we are on a slippery slope to moral chaos." The argument has shifted here: from the defence of literalism to the defence of the authoritative status of biblical commands. The New Atheists run these points together, but they are distinct. One might regard most Old Testament commands as null and void, and yet believe that they can be read literally.

As do the other fallback positions, this one ignores the clear evidence of scripture itself. One of the central controversies throughout the New Testament is the proper relation of Christians to Old Testament law. We see, first, a repeated synthesizing and *focusing* of Old Testament law:

> So whatever you wish that men would do to you, do so to them; for this is the law and the prophets. (Mt 7:12)

> For the whole law is fulfilled in one word, "You shall love your neighbor as yourself." (Gal 5:14)

Remarkably, the more than 600 commands from Old Testament law (Metzger 1965, 48) are synthesized into one great command.

And now we come to a final fallback position: "So Christianity freed us from Old Testament law. But where does the New Testament say we are freed from *New Testament* commands? They must be obeyed and understood literally." Unfortunately for this view, there has always been debate concerning the *scope* of New Testament commands. Do they apply to everyone? Or only to some? Do they apply forever? Or are they directed to a specific context? When Paul advises Timothy: "No longer drink only water, but use a little wine for the sake of your stomach and your frequent ailments" (1 Tim 5:23), is that a universal rule? Would a fundamentalist teetotaller be a contradiction in terms?

Nor are the commands attributed to Jesus himself immune from debates concerning scope. Luther, for example, argues that Jesus's command to "not resist one who is evil" (Mt 5:39) *really* means "Leave the resistance of evil, the administration of justice, and punishment to the one who holds a position in the secular realm." The command thus applies only to ordinary Christians, claims Luther, not to those "holding and administering a secular office or position" (rpt. 1956, 114).[5]

To summarize: there is nothing modern about a non-literal approach to scripture. Throughout history, Christians have approached the Bible in a variety of ways. They have applied non-literal readings to both the Old and the New Testaments, to stories and to commands, including the commands of Jesus himself. I am not saying that this or that approach to the Bible is the only valid one. The argument is historical: whatever one's theological orientation, it cannot be denied that Christians have historically read the Bible in non-literal ways. At the same time, the narrative just presented is critical of biblical literalism, suggesting that those who believe they are engaged in a strictly literal reading do not fully understand what they are up to.

Let us now move beyond the historical argument for a moment. As I cited various Christian authors, many readers will have felt that some of those cited were not *interpreting* scripture so much as running roughshod over it. Some of the allegorical readings in particular strike us today as frankly bizarre.[6] Did early Christian readers engage in "extraordinary trifling" with scripture, as Luther put it? Without endorsing every piece of biblical interpretation presented to this point, we must appreciate what various Christian authors were up to, since the problems with which they grappled remain relevant.

Richard Smith argues that "early Christian writers had recourse to the inner allegorical sense of Scripture," because it was "the only way they could find the divine truth contained in a text that on the surface appeared erroneous" (1968, para. 66.76). Augustine expresses the problem when he exclaims that various Old Testament passages "had been death to me when I took them literally" (rpt. 1961, para. 5.14). Consider Psalm 137. It begins with a haunting lament:

> By the waters of Babylon, there we sat down and wept, when we
>   remembered Zion.
> On the willows there we hung up our lyres.
> For there our captors required of us songs, and our tormentors,
>   mirth, saying, "Sing us one of the songs of Zion!"

The psalm's concluding verse, however, is rather less lyrical. Addressing himself to Babylon, the author declares: "Happy shall he be who takes your little ones and dashes them against the rock!"

(Ps 137:9). Here is Augustine's treatment of the conclusion: "What are the little ones of Babylon? Evil desires at their birth. For there are, who have to fight with inveterate lusts. When lust is born, before evil habit giveth it strength against thee, when lust is little, by no means let it gain the strength of evil habit; when it is little, dash it" (rpt. 1888b, 632). By "spiritualizing" the verse, Augustine neutralizes its celebration of infanticide.

It is striking, given current polemics around evolution, "creationism," and "intelligent design," that one of the risks that Augustine associates with biblical literalism concerns scriptural passages that conflict with known facts:

> A person unfamiliar with the divine word, finding in our sacred books or hearing Christians saying things that seem to contradict scientific truths, could be led to reject the history, the dogma or the morals of religion. One can briefly reply that the sacred authors were well aware of the true shape of the heavens, but that the Holy Spirit, who spoke through them, did not want to reveal to people knowledge that would be of no help to their salvation. (rpt. 1866, 2.9)

Biblical passages, Augustine goes on, must be interpreted so as not to contradict existing opinions on issues such as the shape of the heavens, so long as these opinions are "established on solid reasons." For Augustine literalism poses a risk, *not* to science or scientific freedom, but to faith itself. Perhaps this is still the case.

Unless we believe, then, that God was concerned with teaching humanity scientific truths, there is no reason to expect scientific accuracy from inspiration. As Aquinas would later put it, "those things which cannot pertain to salvation are outside the matter of prophecy" (*Truth*, q. 12, a. 2). Does this mean that biblical statements that contradict scientific truths are thereby "false"? No: in everyday practice we recognize that a true statement need not be true in those respects unrelated to its purpose. Imagine that I tell you: "Last night, I sat by the river and watched the sun go down." If at sunset I was in fact drinking in the local pub with friends, my claim would clearly be false. But my statement is *not* rendered false by the fact that the sun does not in fact "go down," because no adherence to a particular astronomical theory was intended by my statement. Jürgen Habermas argues that to understand a statement, "the interpreter has to be familiar with the conditions of its validity" (1984, 115). If you think that Copernican astronomy renders my statement invalid, you simply haven't *understood* what I was saying.

Thus, early Christian readers did not turn to non-literal interpretations of scripture on a whim, they were driven to it. If, suggests Augustine, you can make sense of a passage through a literal reading, more power to you. "But if there is no way in which we can understand what has been written in a manner that is pious and worthy of God without believing that these things have been set before us in figures and in enigmas, we have the apostolic authority by which so many enigmas from the books of the Old Testament are solved" (1991, 2.2).

A final caution is in order. Christians not given to a "fundamentalist" approach to scripture may assume that their own approach is necessarily more humane and tolerant. Scriptural literalism, we like to believe, is at the root of religious hatred. It is true that Christian writers often turned to the "spiritual" interpretation of scripture to avoid the barbarity of a literal reading, as we saw with Augustine's treatment of Psalm 137. Non-literal interpretations, however, can also be a good vehicle for hatred and prejudice. Consider the first line of the book of Psalms:

Blessed is the man who walks not in the counsel of the wicked.

The phrase does not seem particularly resistant to a strictly literal understanding, nor particularly frightening when read literally. But recall Luther's claim that "this means that the Lord Jesus made no concessions to the designs of the Jews." There is nothing benign about this non-literal interpretation. Another example concerns one of the most disturbing verses in the Bible:

Now go and smite Am'alek, and utterly destroy all that they have; do not spare them, but kill both man and woman, infant and suckling, ox and sheep, camel and ass. (1 Sam 15:3)

A literal reading might simply have said: at one point in history, for who knows what reason, God told his people to commit genocide. But another type of reading allows people to draw dangerous analogies. Ronald Bainton records how early New Englanders saw themselves "as the New Israel of God commissioned to subdue the Indians as the Amalekites." In 1689, Cotton Mather urged the colonists to attack "Amalek annoying this Israel in the Wilderness." And a 1757 sermon from one James Cogswell reminded the faithful that "God was exceedingly displeased with Saul ... for not entirely destroying Amalek" (qtd. in Bainton 1960, 167–9). Not to commit genocide against the natives, it appears, manifested a lack of piety.

This non-literal reading of scripture was anything but benign. Massachusetts settler Captain John Underhill depicted a battle in which some four hundred natives, "men, women, and children," were massacred. The sight was "doleful" for some of the young soldiers: "to see so many souls lie gasping on the ground so thick in some places, that you could hardly pass along." No matter, declared Underhill: "David's war" shows that "we had sufficient light from the word of God for our proceedings" (1638).

4. Conclusion

This chapter has challenged two key New Atheist claims: that there is an obvious relation between "serious" belief and violent intolerance, and that scriptural literalism is a central component of serious belief, one jettisoned only in modern times. Various considerations were advanced against the first claim: violence may spring from uncertainty rather than certainty; it may require a *liberation* from long-standing certainties (e.g., that the killing of innocents is wrong); violence can generate the certainty that justifies it; and, finally, the production of violence on the scale of 9/11 should be seen as a gradual process in which initial beliefs lead a person into new organizational contexts, which generate new beliefs, and so on through various iterations. The second claim, for its part, was dismissed on grounds of historical inaccuracy.

Thus: (a) the relation between religious seriousness and violence is at least an open question, not at all settled in the way the New Atheists assume; (b) the New Atheist claim regarding literalism is simply incorrect. Not all readers will be willing to accept these conclusions, of course. Someone who did not wish to relinquish any piece of New Atheist dogma might argue that our review of the historical record is beside the point: all we have shown is that there have been non-literalist wishy-washy believers throughout the history of Christianity. One could, I suppose, claim this, though to do so one must dismiss Aquinas, Augustine, Luther, *and the New Testament authors themselves*, as wishy-washy Christians.

Even among readers who are not bloody-minded and dogmatic, my argument from the historical record may not fully persuade, for a simple psychological reason. Philosophers of science such as Thomas Kuhn often argue that theories are not refuted by facts alone: they can only be replaced by more satisfying theories (1970, 77). So perhaps we can hasten the demise of the New Atheist understanding of religious seriousness by suggesting an alternative.

In his *Confessions*, Augustine recalls Jesus's declaration that upon the twin commands to love God and neighbour "depend all the law and the prophets" (Mt 22:40). Augustine asks: "Since I believe in these commandments and confess them with all my heart, how can it harm me" to interpret a scriptural passage in one of "several ways, all of which may yet be true? How can it harm me if I understand the writer's meaning in a different sense from that in which another understands it?" (*Confessions*, 12.18). Once one is well grounded, the diversity of possible interpretations of scripture is something to be celebrated, rather than lamented: "If I were called upon to write a book which was to be vested with the highest authority, I should prefer to write it in such a way that a reader could find re-echoed in my words whatever truths he was able to apprehend. I would rather write in this way than impose a single true meaning" (12.31). This suggests that the New Atheist claim regarding scriptural literalism has things exactly backwards: perhaps it takes a very *serious* approach to faith, one that focuses on Christianity's central commandment, to be relaxed about interpretations of scripture. So long, that is, as interpretations do not lose sight of what is truly central.

Generalizing from Christianity to all religions, one might argue that serious believers strive to understand just what is central to their faith and what is secondary, and to shape their lives ever more fully around those central elements. The critic might complain that this view of serious belief leaves us with no simple external markers of seriousness. That is, if serious belief is defined by an ongoing quest to shape one's life according to the central elements of one's faith, rather than by one's willingness to murder "infidels" or threaten abortion providers, it is not easy for an outside observer to figure out just who is serious and who is not. No matter: for the believer, the point of "getting serious" is not to make life easier for social scientists or pamphleteers seeking to draw group portraits of committed believers.

As we conclude this part of the book, I remind the reader of some unfinished business. This chapter has critiqued the New Atheist portrait of serious belief. I have yet to critique the defenders' portrait of serious atheism. That is a rather more complicated task, to which we will turn in chapters 6 and 7. First, though, we will examine the efforts of the New Atheists to articulate a post-religious ethics.

part two

Life Together

chapter five

New Atheist Ethics

One of the important challenges facing the dream of a world without religion was articulated by Dostoyevsky's Ivan Karamazov: if there is no God, is everything permitted? After examining various tactics by which New Atheists occasionally try to brush away the problem of ethics, this chapter will examine their attempts to address Dostoyevsky's concern. As it is the most fully elaborated attempt, I will focus on Sam Harris's "scientific" ethics.

This chapter does not argue against the possibility of a "post-religious ethics." Indeed, there is a sense in which we absolutely *must* articulate and defend such an ethics, one that can appeal to all types of citizens in our pluralistic society. The argument here is simply that we face ethical challenges in our society and world that are not easily met, and that certainly have not been met by the New Atheists themselves.

1. Avoidance Strategies

Three strategies are deployed by the New Atheists to avoid confronting the challenge of ethics: Greeting-card morality, the "Vice is virtue" ruse; and Trust in the evolving Zeitgeist.

Greeting-card morality. Even in this age of irony, one can still find greeting cards that express uplifting sentiments. Greeting-card morality resembles them. It is the morality of the "decent chap":

he discovers certain sentiments within himself, or reads them somewhere, and takes them as self-evident. He doesn't trouble to ask whether others would have good reasons to share or reject those sentiments. Dawkins, for examples, cites Einstein's claim that "there is one thing we do know: that man is here for the sake of other men" (2006, 209). To which a cynic can reply: and how exactly do we "know" this? Dawkins also declares that "the knowledge that we have only one life should make it all the more precious" (2006, 361). Yes, it certainly makes *my* life seem more precious to me. But it need not generate much concern for the lives of others.

Harris also offers a greeting-card sentiment based on our mortality. Everyone we know, he declares in his earnest epilogue to *The End of Faith*, will one day die. Each "will suffer the loss of his friends and family." So "Why would anyone want to be anything but kind to them in the meantime?" (2004, 226). Why indeed! For the same reasons that people have always been unkind: to take someone's property or their spouse, to assert one's superiority, to avenge oneself.

Vice is virtue. Hitchens believes that many apparent vices are actually good for us. The Ten Commandments foolishly tell us not to covet: envy is a good thing, as it "can lead to emulation and ambition" (2007, 100). "Cupidity and avarice," declares Hitchens, "are the spur to economic development" (214), in support of which he offers one of Adam Smith's most famous statements: "It is not from the benevolence of the butcher, the brewer, or the baker that we expect our dinner, but from their regard to their own interest" (rpt. 1937, 14).

It is unfortunate that Hitchens did not read more of Smith, who might have cured him of a disturbingly naive understanding of ethics and economics. Smith argued that self-interest, when provided with a strong scaffolding of ethical norms, could promote social goods. But he repeatedly stressed that unbridled self-interest had inflicted appalling calamities.[1] The Dutch colonial companies, he remarks at one point, had engaged in what we would today call genocide, for *business purposes* (rpt. 1937, 601).

Like the Bible, the *Wealth of Nations* is a long book. Many of the self-proclaimed disciples of each work are more fond of invoking some fragment from their favoured text than of reading it.[2] But even someone who has not read Smith should recognize that drug pushers and human smugglers are well acquainted with the "cupidity and avarice" that Hitchens lauds. Unchecked by strong ethical norms, self-interest is calamitous. The ethical challenge cannot be ignored by pretending that vice is virtue.

Trust in the evolving Zeitgeist. For Dawkins, there is no need to construct a post-religious ethical system: the evolving spirit of the age will take care of that. Dawkins is sure that this Zeitgeist is moving in the right direction, and will continue to do so. We can observe evidence of ethical evolution in the rapid spread of women's suffrage, and in growing acceptance of sexual and racial equality (2006, 265–7). People who seemed "progressive" in their time, such as Thomas Huxley or Lincoln, would seem racist in our own day, proof of how far we have advanced. We also see "a steadily shifting standard of what is morally acceptable" in war, to the extent that even Hitler "would not have stood out in the time of Caligula or Genghis Khan" (268).[3]

All these positive developments of the moral Zeitgeist "certainly have not come from religion" (2006, 270). One important source of moral development, Dawkins argues, is "the increased understanding that each of us shares a common humanity, with members of other races and with the other sex – both deeply unbiblical ideas that come from biological science, especially evolution" (271). Far from being a threat to all morality, as many conservatives had assumed, Darwinism turns out to be a wellspring of ethical progress. The spread of such scientific ideas encourages Dawkins to make a brave claim: "Over the longer timescale, the progressive trend is unmistakable *and it will continue*" (2006, 271; emphasis added).[4]

The argument is a fine example of the naive optimism that has weakened the thought of many thinkers over recent centuries. It is incumbent upon the sceptic as much as the believer to acknowledge the ambiguities and dangers of his preferred sources of guidance and inspiration. Does Dawkins truly believe that "biological science, especially evolution" has produced only positive moral effects? Nietzsche took aim at such naivety over a century ago, when he lambasted German theologian David Strauss for having hailed Darwin as one of "mankind's greatest benefactors," yet failing to offer a "seriously constructed ethical system, based upon Darwin's teaching." Such a system, Nietzsche insisted, would have "established a moral code for life out of *bellum omnium contra omnes* [the war of all against all] and the privileges of the strong" (rpt. 2004, 45–6).

Not for nothing was one of the most ruthless political philosophies of modernity labelled "social Darwinism." Dawkins has clearly been exposed to the genre, but fails to acknowledge its source of inspiration: as evidence of our evolving Zeitgeist, he offers up a remarkably ugly quote from H.G. Wells, considered "a progressive in his own time" (2006, 270). Wells dreams of a utopia that will "make the multiplication of those who fall behind a certain standard of social efficiency unpleasant and difficult, and it will have cast aside any coddling laws to save adult men from themselves" (1901, 340). The statement's roots in social Darwinism are clear, but Dawkins passes over this in silence. This is not the only evidence of this sort that Dawkins prefers to ignore. I noted in chapter 2 that Dawkins cites historian Alan Bullock as support for the claim that Hitler was a lifelong Catholic, omitting Bullock's comment that Hitler "detested" Christian ethics, which he considered "a rebellion against the natural law of selection by struggle and the survival of the fittest" (1962, 389). This does not make a Nazi out of Darwin, any more than Nazi use of anti-Semitic passages in the Gospel of John makes a Nazi out of Jesus. But it reminds us once again that any influential school of thought will be put to a wide variety of uses, with little regard to the intentions of that school's founders.[5]

And has the ethical Zeitgeist truly evolved in an unambiguously positive direction? Certainly, in the developed world, there is probably less discrimination today against women, gays, or members of minority ethnic and racial groups. "We," collectively speaking, may be nicer to others than before, *so long as they have money*.[6]

That is, our society tolerates discrimination less than it once did, but our willingness to alleviate the suffering caused by poverty remains fairly primitive, and may even have atrophied in recent decades. Nor does it seem that the "global village" promised by the explosion of communications technology has led to a deepening of our compassion for the poor majority of our world. Against the claim of an exquisitely evolved sensibility, our failure to act in Rwanda and in Darfur, even while the means of communication made clear just what was happening there, would suggest that we have hardened our hearts to an unprecedented degree.

In his *Moral Landscape*, Harris claims that "those of us who live in the developed world are becoming increasingly disturbed by our capacity to do one another harm. We are less tolerant of 'collateral damage' in times of war – undoubtedly because we now see images of it" (2010, 175). The very opposite may well be true: we seem to have hardened our hearts to the point that even televised images of human suffering have little impact on support for foreign military adventures. There is simply no evidence to suggest, for example, that decline in the American public's support for the war on Iraq was influenced by the suffering of the *Iraqi* people.

Indeed, modernity has been prolific in creating theoretical justifications for our callousness. Expressions of social Darwinism generally play on the theme that much human suffering should not be alleviated, as it is a necessary price for humanity's progress, or at least survival. This is a modern theme, though it predates Darwin, as shown by Scrooge's dismissive "If they would rather die, they had better do it, and decrease the surplus population." Scrooge was a mouthpiece for the political economy of his time, the new "secular religion" through which "compassion was removed from the hearts," as historian Karl Polanyi put it (1957, 102). Many close observers of post–Second World War institutions such as the World Bank or the International Monetary Fund would suggest that though our language has become much more guarded since the time of Scrooge or Nassau Senior,[7] our actual practice has not progressed much. Even were one to point to our quite limited interest in alleviating world poverty as a sign that the Zeitgeist is moving in the right direction, it would be dangerous to project such a trend into the future. What will happen to Dawkins's Zeitgeist, one must wonder, if we are truly entering an age of multiple ecological crises?

So neither greeting-card sentiments, nor the confusion of vice and virtue, nor the benign evolution of the Zeitgeist will allow us to avoid the problem of ethics.

2. Harris's Science of Good and Evil

Of the New Atheists, Sam Harris offers the most elaborate attempt to offer a post-religious foundation for ethics. Though, as we saw, he too can lapse into greeting-card morality, he does acknowledge the key challenge: "Once we abandon our belief in a rule-making God, the question of *why* a given action is good or bad becomes a matter of debate." Fortunately, "A science of good and evil" is within our reach (2004, 170). Let us examine the foundations of Harris's ethical science.[8]

For Harris, "Science is science because it represents our most committed effort to verify that our statements about the world are true (or at least not false). We do this by observation and experiment within the context of a theory" (2004, 75–6). One could quibble about this, but let us accept it as a working definition of science.

Can one then have a scientific ethics? Yes, claims Harris, "once we realize that questions of right and wrong are really questions about the happiness and suffering of sentient creatures" (2004, 170). The "really" is important: ethics does not merely *involve* considerations of happiness and suffering, it is simply *about* happiness and suffering: "For ethics to matter to us, the happiness and suffering of others must matter to us" (185).

Happiness and religion. This starting-point, oddly, seriously undermines Harris's attack on religion. "One of the most robust findings of happiness research," notes economist Richard Layard, is that "people who believe in God are happier" (2003). "World Values Survey" data suggest that the difference in self-reported life satisfaction between those who agree that "God is very important to their lives" and those who don't is roughly the same as the life-satisfaction difference between people in the middle of the income distribution and those in the top 10 per cent (Helliwell 2002). This is striking, given that in the United States, for example, those in the top decile of the income distribution earn more than triple the income of those in the 5th decile (US Census Bureau 2000).

Let us be cynical for a moment. Even if someone could prove that faith were a total delusion, anyone whose starting point is an ethic of happiness would be unable to condemn faith. Indeed, one might even say that happiness based on religion is particularly valuable: compared to the alternative of increased income and consumption, religious belief doesn't consume fossil fuels or produce much in the way of greenhouse gasses. The clear inference is that, for an ethics based on happiness, the ideal of ideals would be a religious belief that affords its adherents the happiness "fix" associated with religion in general, but which avoids doctrines that might spark violence.

Given that they view religion as a pathology, how do the New Atheists deal with the empirical link between religion and happiness? One strategy is simply to ignore it: "There may be statistical evidence bearing on the relationship between happiness and belief (or unbelief), but I doubt if it is a strong effect," declares Dawkins, clearly disinclined to examine the evidence that "may" exist (2006, 353).[9] Having ruled out an examination of real evidence, Dawkins is then free to offer "evidence" more congenial to his outlook: "A senior nurse of my acquaintance," he assures us, "has noticed over the years that the individuals who are most afraid of death are the religious ones" (357).[10]

Another strategy is to declare by fiat that religion simply *must* make people unhappy. There is a "very obvious and highly unmentionable" link between "religious faith and mental disorder," declares Hitchens (2007, 53). Small wonder, given that "the three great monotheisms teach people to think abjectly of themselves, as miserable and guilty sinners before an angry and jealous god" (73). The "fixation with death" promoted by religion, suggests Onfray, "generates every kind of risky behavior, suicidal impulse, and self-destructive conduct" (2007, 66).

A third strategy is to argue that any happiness promoted by religion is illegitimate: "If the prospect of getting taken up to paradise generates joy, it is the mindless joy of a baby picked up from his crib" (Onfray 2007, 96). Let us examine this line of response more carefully, as it points to a challenge facing any "scientific" ethics. The assumption is that, if happiness is to be our ethical yardstick, it must be subject to some sort of limiting condition. One might say, with Onfray, that legitimate happiness is not "mindless," that we must keep our "feet on the ground, in contact with the one true world" (2007, 96). Let us summarize such limiting conditions on happiness with the simple injunction, that one must not "live a lie." We will bypass the question of whether faith is a lie, and ask instead: where does such a limiting condition come from? What is its justification? The condition is based on a vision of what constitutes a good and dignified human life. Such visions are an unavoidable element in our evaluations of real or possible social arrangements. We all carry around such visions, and it is in their name that we are repelled by certain images of real or possible societies.

But can anyone give a strictly "evidence-based" justification for any particular vision of a good human life? Harris is, after all, trying to build a strictly "scientific" ethics. So what precisely is the "observation and experiment" that might support the injunction not to live a lie?[11] Can we base the limiting condition upon objective evidence? Supposing we attempt this, what form would the argument take? One would probably attempt to justify the condition on the basis of some other value, for example, circling back to a claim of the form "living a lie won't make you happy in the long run." But we introduced our rejection of living a lie as a *limiting condition* upon an ethics of happiness. Now we find that the condition is dependent for its validity upon happiness itself. And what if the claim that living a lie won't yield happiness is empirically disproved?[12] Would we then be willing to say, "Oh well, I suppose it's OK to live a lie after all"?

We can argue about our visions of a good human life, and we can provide reasons for or against a particular vision, but we will not settle debates between competing visions by a conclusive appeal to evidence. We can rationally talk about, argue over, reflect upon, the most important questions in our lives. But we cannot expect our answers to those questions to attain the status of scientific truth. Thus, Harris's attempt to build a science of ethics has failed from the outset. He must either

(1) accept the empirical finding that religious belief is associated with happiness, and conclude that an ethics of happiness would do well to promote religion; or

(2) introduce a limiting condition on the ethics of happiness, one that itself is highly contestable, and cannot be verified by "observation and experiment."[13]

There is an irony here. The religion-happiness link might lead an unbiased utilitarian to promote religion. Many serious believers, however, would be dismayed at this prospect. They would argue that the *point* of faith is not simply to make people happy. While the believer's ultimate goal may promise perfect happiness, one does not move towards that goal by pursuing happiness directly, and *certainly* not by shaping religion in order to maximize its happiness "pay-off."

Love and happiness. The point of Harris's science of ethics is to show that we can get along just fine without religion. Harris argues that we don't need divine guidance to know what constitutes right action. All we need do is promote happiness. As we have seen, this claim leads him into a dead end. Harris also believes that science will provide us all with strong reasons to want to behave ethically. Let us consider this second dimension of his scientific ethics.

"Our common humanity," says Harris, "is reason enough to protect our fellow human beings from coming to harm" (2004, 106). To answer the person who wonders why "common humanity" should lead one to make sacrifices for others, Harris brings love into the picture. Love, says Harris, "is largely a matter of wishing that others experience happiness rather than suffering" (186). Since ethics is also centred upon happiness and suffering in Harris's framework, to love someone is to wish to behave ethically towards them. Now "most of us come to feel that love is more conducive to happiness, both our own and that of others, than hate" (187). Because love and ethics are identified, "we can hypothesize" that a person's happiness will increase as they become more ethical (191). Thus, one can wish to become more loving and compassionate "for purely selfish reasons" (191). Let us call this the "love-happiness claim." It asserts: (a) To be ethical towards others is to love them and (b) This leads to one's own happiness.

Harris has articulated an important truth, but it is only a partial truth. Because it is partial, his approach represents a regression relative to the ethical consciousness developed within the Bible. That ethical action promotes our own well-being even in this life is *one* aspect of the Bible's message: "I have been young, and now am old; yet I have not seen the righteous forsaken" (Ps 37:25). The language differs from that of Harris, but the underlying claim is the same: even leaving aside considerations of "eternal rewards," it is in our interest to behave ethically.

But scripture also challenges this comfortable message. The book of Job, above all, answers the claim that being just and being happy are neatly linked, and that our suffering is somehow proportioned to our own sins.[14] The world-weary book of Ecclesiastes also comments: "In my vain life I have seen everything; there is a righteous man who perishes in his righteousness, and there is a wicked man who prolongs his life in his evil-doing" (Eccles 7:15).

There is *some* truth within both of these positions. On the one hand, empirical studies show that friendship and family are important for happiness (Lane 2000, 80; Helliwell 2002, 40). This would indicate a link between caring for others and being happy. We also know that much of what we suffer can be of our own doing. The Deuterocanonical book of Sirach comments that "mean injustice withers the soul" (Sir 14:9), and we can probably all think of people whose souls seem to have been withered by chronic selfishness, which is no recipe for happiness.

And yet this is not the whole story. External events can crash in upon us, bringing sadness to even the most caring person. Someone's happiness can be destroyed, for example, when she is caught up in a political whirlwind for which she is in no way responsible. One might answer: "Of course there will always be events beyond one's control, so there are no guarantees of happiness. But not everything is beyond your control. You can choose your own approach to life, and to the extent that you behave ethically, that you care for others, you increase your chances of being happy."

Again, this optimistic claim is true to a point. But it ignores the great costs to acting justly in an unjust world. Those who try to expand their radius of love and care, who try to behave in an ethical and caring way towards a broader circle, often pay a heavy price for their love. We regularly read about murdered human-rights campaigners, imprisoned environmentalists, tortured democracy activists. These martyrs have tried to do justice for their fellow citizens, for those who are unjustly persecuted, for future generations. They are not victims who simply *happen* to be good people, but people who suffer *because* they are good.

It is no good here to appeal to what Harris calls "rarefied" happiness (2004, 192) to suggest that the murdered human-rights activist's commitment yielded her profound satisfaction, of a type not understood by ordinary people. For the purposes of Harris's argument, the love-happiness link must serve as a motivator for ordinary people here-and-now, not merely for a special few who have privileged insights into the nature of rarefied happiness.

Harris has in effect articulated an ethics for a world (a) that is already just and (b) in which, for some reason or other, no threats to justice can emerge.[15] In such a world, there could be a straightforward link between loving others and enjoying life. Because that world would already be just, love would not require that we fight injustice, that we run risks and make great sacrifices. Love would merely involve an ongoing stream of small acts of kindness and tenderness, and such virtue would indeed be its own reward.[16]

But in our unjust world, ethical action is not always so easy and gratifying. In our real world, just what will motivate us to run serious risks in the name of justice? Harris dwells on the *barriers* to identification with other people, particularly barriers created by religion. He assumes that if we remove those barriers, it will be natural for people to care for total strangers.[17] But why?

Harris believes that the course of events will solve this problem for us. He allows that religion played a role in the past in uniting communities, but suggests that no such help is needed today, because the modern world is "already united, at least potentially, by economic, environmental, political and epidemiological necessity" (2004, 25).[18] This is a grave error. The objective necessity for united action need not generate a subjective awareness of that necessity, much less the willingness to act on that awareness. Indeed, precisely the opposite may occur. Benjamin Barber has argued that the pressure of globalization is helping to provoke an *intensification* of narrow identities (1992).[19] Rather than generating an increased recognition of our "common humanity," our growing *involuntary* interdependence can lead to violent reactions.[20]

The foregoing argument in no way implies that one cannot be "good without God." The activists mentioned above, who suffer for their commitment to human rights, democracy, or the environment, need not be motivated by any religious belief. My point is rather that such goodness does not arise merely from a "subtraction" of faith from their make-up. It should be obvious, to anyone who pays attention to the evidence all around us, that a mere absence of faith does not provide people with a powerful desire to do justice.

An authoritarian science of ethics. Harris vigorously rejects any questioning of the love-happiness link. He explicitly exempts the claim from the test of "observation and experiment" that is supposed to be the hallmark of science: "Like so much that we know about ourselves, claims of this sort need not be validated by a controlled study." They are rather "a hypothesis to be tested in the laboratory of one's life" (2004, 192). But everyday life is not a reliable "laboratory." As we have just noted, the link between love and happiness may seem plausible within everyday life, yet break down entirely outside that narrow sphere.

Having decided that the love-happiness claim need not be tested, Harris suggests that those who reject the claim probably have no business taking part in a serious ethical discussion: "Some people can't make heads or tails of the assertion that the passage of time might be relative to one's frame of reference. This prevents them from taking part in any serious discussion of physics. People who can see no link between love and happiness may find themselves in the same position with respect to ethics" (2004, 187). In his repeated analogies between the natural sciences and his own stab at an ethical science, Harris is seeking to expel many points of view, *and most people*, from the realm of ethical discourse:

> Sustained inquiry in the moral sphere will force convergence of our various belief systems in the way that it has in every other science – that is, *among those who are adequate to the task* ... When was the last time that someone was criticized for not "respecting" another person's unfounded beliefs about physics or history? The same rules should apply to ethical, spiritual, and religious beliefs as well. (2004, 175–6; emphasis added)

Our future well-being, Harris asserts, requires "finding approaches to ethics and to spiritual experience that make no appeal to faith, and broadcasting this knowledge to everyone" (2004, 224). The image is telling: we are being offered a world divided on ethical matters between the few broadcasters and the many receivers. In Harris's utopia, ethical reasoning will for most people be a spectator sport.

Harris's hope for a "convergence of our various belief systems" under the guidance of ethical experts such as himself recalls nineteenth-century French sociologist Auguste Comte's search for a "scientific dogma whose common acceptance would bring forth a new social order" (Gilson 1937, 257). Like Harris's experts, Comte's "servants of Humanity come, fittingly, to take over the general direction of earthly matters" (1890, 5). Nor is Harris the only New Atheist to indulge in such elitism. Dennett too is attracted by this vision: "My central policy recommendation is that *we* gently, firmly educate the people of the world, so that *they* can make truly informed choices about their lives" (2006, 339; emphases added).[21] Indeed, Dennett and his fellow researchers must be prepared to stand guard over democracy itself to ensure the fruits of their work are not misused: "Even if we do the science of religion right (for the first time), we must strenuously guard the integrity of the next process, the boiling down of the complex results of the research into political decisions" (73).

However distasteful all this may seem, one might still have to accept such ethical elitism were the analogy between physics and ethics valid. But it is not. With enough time, someone can be led through the steps to an understanding of relativity. But no amount of time would guarantee that even a reasonably intelligent person would come to share Harris's love-happiness claim, because the claim is not entirely true.

More disturbing still is that Harris's ethical "science" leads him to advocate extreme forms of political control and violence. One of his most vivid critiques of religion is a detailed description of torture under the Inquisition. But it turns out that Harris's own ethical system permits torture. We should not even wring our hands over the torture of innocents, since we kill innocents in war. Indeed, we kill infants in war, but there are no infants at Guantanamo Bay, "just rather scrofulous young men" (2004, 194). This, apparently, changes everything. Harris recognizes that many readers will take exception to his justification of torture: our qualms, he asserts, reflect our "neurological" limitations (199).

As striking as Harris's advocacy of torture is his negation of freedom of belief. Modern democracies have invariably distinguished between behaviour, which is subject to state control, and belief, which is not. Harris rejects this distinction: "Beliefs are scarcely more private than actions are, for every belief is a fount of action *in potentia*" (2004, 44). Because "certain beliefs are *intrinsically* dangerous" (44), we have "simply lost the right to our myths" (48). As an example, Harris suggests that Muslims should not be "free to believe that the Creator of the universe is concerned about hemlines" (46). What do these statements really mean? Is Harris actually suggesting that we should punish people for holding certain beliefs? Yes: "Some propositions are so dangerous that it may even be ethical to kill people for believing them" (52).

So Harris's scientific ethics permit torture, even of innocent people, and the pre-emptive killing of those thought to hold dangerous beliefs.[22] A final characteristic of his ethical science is that it rules out all restraints on the way we wage war: "When your enemy has no scruples, your own scruples become another weapon in his hand" (2004, 202). Because "millions of Muslims around the world" wish to impose a Taliban-like existence upon us, we shouldn't entertain any "qualms over collateral damage" (203). At the extreme, Harris suggests that, should an "Islamist regime" obtain "long-range nuclear weaponry," we might have to "kill tens of millions of innocent civilians in a single day" through a nuclear first strike. This would be "an unthinkable crime" and an "unconscionable act of self-defense."[23] Yet "it may be the only course of action available to us, given what Islamists believe" (129).[24]

Reflections. I noted at the start of this chapter the need to confront Ivan Karamazov's claim that everything is permitted if there is no God. Harris set out to show that the rejection of religion does not entail moral chaos. Ironically, though, he has ended up affirming that, at least in waging war against those he considers his enemies, everything is indeed permitted. How does a thinker who wishes to be reasonable and humane end up holding such positions? Two observations may shed light on this process.

First, Harris has fallen into a dangerous dualism. Those whom he labels "our enemies" are quite simply *demonic*. A key manifestation of their demonic quality is the willingness to inflict mass evil with no thought to material or political advantage. Because Islam is a "thoroughgoing cult of death," we can't have a *cold* war with a nuclear Islamist regime (Harris 2004, 123). Such a regime "grows dewy-eyed at the mere mention of paradise," and is thus immune to the conventional deterrence that marked the Cold War (128–9). Harris is so certain of the style of politics that a "devout Muslim" must practise that he somehow fails to notice that no Islamic government in human history has ever committed national suicide.

My second observation draws from fiction. Arthur Koestler's *Darkness at Noon* depicts the fate of one Rubashov, a victim of Stalin's purges. Upon arriving in prison, Rubashov comments that "we have thrown overboard all conventions ... Our sole guiding principle is that of consequent logic ... We are sailing without ethical ballast." Just before his execution, Rubashov recalls these words, and adds: "Perhaps the heart of the evil lay there. Perhaps it did not suit mankind to sail without ballast. And perhaps reason alone was a defective compass, which led one on such a winding, twisted course that the goal finally disappeared in the mist" (1964, 82, 206). The problem with "consequent logic," with trying to deduce all one's actions from a few simple principles, is that if an opening premise is wrong, or is understood incorrectly, or if one error of deduction is made, the final result can be catastrophic.

To guard against runaway "consequent logic," we need *touchstones*: insights, people we trust, gut intuitions, to which we periodically turn. *Everyone*, religious or not, needs such touchstones, because the deduction of our principles of right and wrong from a few simple axioms is a perilous process. In his very ambition to construct an ethical "science," Harris throws away all touchstones. Like Koestler's Rubashov, Harris believes we can advance without "ethical ballast." This is most evident in his discussion of torture. The argument that the torture of innocents may be justified provokes revulsion in most normal people. This revulsion is an alarm bell, a warning that something may have gone horribly wrong with one's chain of deductions. Such moral intuitions are not infallible, but they do constitute ethical ballast, calling us to stop and cast an eye over the course of the argument whenever we have reached a particularly disturbing point in our intellectual wandering. Harris dismisses the alarm bells. As noted, our revulsion around torture is the product of "neurological" limitations (2004, 199). The problem, says Harris, is that we are the products of evolution, and we evolve more slowly than our situation: "Millions of years on the African veldt" (195) make it hard for us to appreciate the soundness of the case for torture.[25]

Harris's runaway deductivism might be contrasted with the search for what John Rawls calls "reflective equilibrium." In this approach, deductions from general principles are tested against our "considered judgments," those "in which our moral capacities are most likely to be displayed without distortion" (1971, 47). Thus, for Rawls, considered judgments such as "the belief in religious toleration and the rejection of slavery" act as "provisional fixed points" in our thinking (1996, 8). Something like Rawls's approach has long been recommended by a variety of thinkers, Aristotle (*Ethics* 1179a) and Adam Smith (rpt. 2009, 357) among them.

Yet neither is Harris's approach new. In allowing logical deduction, as he understands it, to trump common sense, Harris has company. J.S. Mill ends his book on Auguste Comte with a comment likening him to Descartes and Leibniz: "They were, of all great scientific thinkers, the most consistent, and for that reason often the most absurd, because they shrunk from no consequences, however contrary to common sense, to which their premises appeared to lead" (1873, 181).

The disturbing direction taken by Harris's ethical "science" suggests that a "post-religious ethics" need not be as unambiguously positive as the New Atheists assume. But perhaps Harris is simply a confused thinker, and his violent and authoritarian "science of ethics" is entirely unrepresentative of New Atheist ethics. If so, it is striking that Dawkins, Dennett, and Hitchens, all of whom have read him, offer not a whisper of criticism of Harris's endorsement of torture and nuclear strikes on civilian populations, nor of any other aspect of Harris's work, for that matter. Dawkins is rightly outraged by the case of an Afghan man sentenced to die for "certain *thoughts*," which he held "internally and privately" (2006, 287). But he has nothing to say about Harris's assertion that it is legitimate to kill someone for their beliefs.

This is but one example of the clannishness of the New Atheists. They acknowledge each other in their prefaces,[26] draw upon each other's arguments,[27] and praise each other's work.[28] Where one might expect respectful disagreement at the very least, there is none. I cannot believe, for example, that a competent philosopher such as Dennett can possibly accept Harris's simplistic claims about living by evidence, or Dawkins's supposed proof of the non-existence of God. But he keeps his thoughts to himself on such matters, following, it seems, the "enemy of my enemy is my friend" principle.[29]

We saw in chapter 1 that the New Atheists accuse "moderate" believers of providing ideological cover for intolerant fundamentalists. Dennett, for example, argues the need to expose religious fanatics, "from the inside," and adds: "Any religious person who is not actively and publicly involved in that effort is shirking a duty" (2006, 301). But are the New Atheists willing to shoulder an analogous responsibility? Are they willing publicly to declare that it is just as reprehensible for a fellow critic of religion to propose a nuclear attack on a civilian population as it would be for an Iranian leader?[30]

The foregoing observations concerning the clannishness of the New Atheists do not apply to Onfray: his original book dates from 2005, and I find no evidence that he has read the other works. But Onfray does provide another view of the possible trajectory of post-religious ethics, and it is not terribly encouraging.

3. Onfray's Post-Christian Ethics

The epigraph for Onfray's book is a long citation from Nietzsche. As Hans Küng notes, Nietzsche rejected a "careless, irresponsible atheism" (1981, 371). Nietzsche insisted that his contemporaries had failed to grasp the implications of the "death of God": they were "still too much under the impression of the *initial consequences* of this event ... a new and scarcely describable kind of light, relief, exhilaration, encouragement, dawn" (rpt. 1974, 280).

Onfray identifies his own project with that of Nietzsche: "Atheism is not an end in itself. Do away with God, yes, but then what? Another morality, a new ethic, values never before thought of because unthinkable" (2007, 34). Much atheist thought has failed to take that next step, Onfray argues. Those who try to deduce values from "a utilitarian and pragmatic viewpoint," generally the case with the other New Atheists, Onfray dismisses as "Christian atheists" (56).

And what will a society grounded in Onfray's "new ethic" look like? It will be a society without law, because "the law *always* supports the ruling caste's domination over the masses" (2007, 148). Onfray's post-Christian society will be free of a number of other social practices as well: "Family, marriage, monogamy, fidelity – all of them variations on the theme of castration" (105). One must assume that fidelity to one's children will also be "transcended," which will certainly carry us into uncharted territory.

Onfray's new world will be humane, he believes, because it will have outgrown the "magical thinking" embodied in the "principle of free will" (2007, 51).[31] Our entire "judicial logic" flows from the book of Genesis account of the fall of Adam and Eve, because it tells "the story of a man who is free, and therefore responsible for his acts" (49). And so we imprison the person who rapes children, under the supposition that he is free. We would never lock up someone "diagnosed with a brain tumor," yet those who rape children are no more responsible for their "fixation" than the cancer patient for his tumour (50).

For all his professed radicalism, Onfray is following a well-trodden path here. Writing in 1930, Bertrand Russell also identified belief in free will as a hangover from Christianity, and drew the logical implication: "A man who is suffering from plague has to be imprisoned until he is cured, although nobody thinks him wicked. The same thing should be done with a man who suffers from a propensity to commit forgery; but there should be no more idea of guilt in the one case than in the other" (1957, 41). This sounds very enlightened, but critics as diverse as C.S. Lewis and Michel Foucault have warned that this more "humanitarian" approach can license domination without limits. In his 1954 essay "The Humanitarian Theory of Punishment," Lewis warned that, in this approach, "each one of us, from the moment he breaks the law, is deprived of the rights of a human being" (rpt. 1970, 288). Russell's reference to society's response to a plague illustrates this: the victim "has to be imprisoned until he is cured." And if he is never cured? Then he must remain imprisoned for ever, through no fault of his own. This reflects no consideration of justice, but a utilitarian calculation.[32] Once one draws the analogy between crime and disease, it logically follows that the treatment even of the petty thief may well have no end. Nor will the "patient" experience the "cure" as any more humane than the "punishment" it replaces: "To undergo all those assaults on my personality which modern psychotherapy knows how to deliver; to be re-made after some pattern of 'normality' hatched in a Viennese laboratory to which I never professed allegiance; to know that this process will never end until either my captors have succeeded or I grown wise enough to cheat them with apparent success – who cares whether this is called Punishment or not?" (Lewis rpt. 1970, 290).

Light years removed from C.S. Lewis in many respects, philosopher Michel Foucault nevertheless was equally suspicious of the "humanitarian" claims of penal reformers. One sinister implication is that law's binary division between the permitted and the forbidden is supplanted by the "norm," total conformity to which may be demanded within various social institutions. Under the rule of law, what is not forbidden is permitted. But where the "norm" reigns, everything must be done *just right*, as in that most humane of institutions, the boot camp. So the replacement of punishment by a zeal for "correction" can "make punishable the most fine-grained fractions of behavior" (1975, 210).

So Onfray's "enlightened" approach to crime and responsibility can lead a society to extreme forms of repression. But as Stanley Fish has argued, a "slippery slope" argument of the sort I am using here "assumes that there is nothing in place, no underbrush, to stop the slide" (1994, 130). Perhaps society will benefit from "underbrush" that halts our slide towards repression. But what sort of underbrush might be available? Conscience? We have already seen what enlightened thinkers such as Harris can do to that phenomenon. Perhaps we would be saved by a sense of the inherent dignity of every human being. But will that sense survive the ethical progress for which the New Atheists yearn? Dawkins argues that the "absolutist," who insists on "granting humans unique and special status *because they are human*," is ignoring "the fact of evolution," which demonstrates "our evolutionary continuity with chimpanzees and, more distantly, with every species on the planet" (2006, 300–1). Dawkins, whose vision of the ethical Zeitgeist suffers from Panglossian optimism, probably assumes that erasing the line between the human and the non-human will lead to a "levelling up" in our treatment of other species. Given our ecological situation and the concentration of wealth and power in today's world, however, there are good reasons to expect an ethical "levelling down." So a belief in the inherent dignity of our fellow human beings may not be robust enough to halt a slide towards repression in Onfray's post-religious utopia.

A casual reader of Onfray's book might view as unfair the points made here. Unlike Harris, Onfray shrinks from pursuing his train of thought to its grim conclusion. So a careful reading is required in order to grasp the more chilling implications of his approach. Consider, for example, a crucial question: just who would be subject to therapeutic treatment in Onfray's post-religious world? He does not explicitly say, but there is cause for concern, since his conception of disease, which already embraces the cancer patient and the rapist of children, also extends to the realm of *thought*.[33]

Onfray offers an entire chapter titled: "The Pauline contamination." After listing Paul's New Testament travels, Onfray comments: "Everywhere, he contaminated. Soon Paul's disease infected the whole body of the empire" (2007, 138). Onfray, who asserts the atheist's freedom from the "magical thinking" that afflicts believers (16), himself indulges in quasi-magical thought here. How, *concretely*, did Paul "contaminate" the world? It seems that the victims of his contamination were unable to resist the ideas that he transmitted. But why? Onfray does not say.[34]

Such quasi-magical language is not innocent. There is a clear link between the application of the disease metaphor to thought and political authoritarianism. This is nicely illustrated at the outset of Vassilis Vassilikos's novel, Z, in which a fascist Greek general develops the analogy between Communism and "downy mildew" (1996, 6).[35] Am I being unfair to Onfray here? Consider his claim that "the smallest hint of theocracy neutralizes the very essence of democracy" (2007, 177). We see again the danger lurking in metaphors of purity and contamination: democracy is a fragile flower, easily destroyed by the "smallest hint" of impurity. Such thinking has always given cover to those who would abolish democratic freedoms in the name of saving democracy. As an aside, one might ask just what constitutes "the smallest hint of theocracy"? Onfray's book was published in France shortly after a remarkable national debate, in which many claimed that allowing Muslim girls to wear headscarves to school was a threat to the Republic, and an opening to … Islamic theocracy. Democracy, in this view, is a fragile flower indeed!

Onfray is not the only New Atheist to indulge in the dangerous metaphor of contamination. Dennett's work opens with an analogy between the religious believer and an ant whose "brain has been commandeered by a tiny parasite" (2006, 3). Dawkins likens the adoption of belief to "infection by mind viruses" (2006, 176), and elsewhere declares faith "one of the world's great evils, comparable to the smallpox virus but harder to eradicate" (1997). Hitchens goes furthest. In a passage with deeply disturbing overtones, he comments on the Jewish feast of Hanukkah, which in his view celebrates "an absolutely tragic day in human history." When the Maccabees re-established the temple in the second century BC, they were "forcibly restoring Mosaic fundamentalism." Had they *failed*, "the Jewish people might have been the carriers of philosophy instead of arid monotheism": "Here was a poisonous branch that should have been snapped off long ago, or allowed to die out, before it could infect any healthy growth with its junk DNA. But yet we still dwell in its unwholesome, life-killing shadow. And little Jewish children celebrate Hannukah" (2007, 273–5). Hitchens is talking about Judaism rather than Jews, a distinction that not all readers will be inclined to accept. In any case, the comparison of Judaism to a "poisonous branch" that can "infect any healthy growth" is chilling.

We saw that Onfray wishes to pursue a more radical and consistent atheism, to go beyond the mere denial of God's existence to formulate "another morality, a new ethic." We now have some idea what his "new ethic" will look like. And where, in the end, does his supposedly consistent atheism take us? We must, Onfray insists, "de-Christianize secularism, which would benefit immeasurably by emancipating itself still further from Judeo-Christian metaphysics, and which could truly be of service in the wars ahead" (2007, 218). Wars ahead? Which wars are these? Onfray doesn't say. And what would constitute *victory* in these "wars"? On this point, he is more forthcoming. Victory will certainly *not* usher in an age of mutual tolerance and equality between believers and unbelievers, as Onfray makes clear in the last pages of his work. If we accept equality between the believer and "the thinker who deconstructs the manufacture of belief, the building of a myth, the creation of a fable," says Onfray, "then let's stop thinking" (2007, 218–19).[36]

Some readers may be tempted to dismiss Onfray as a kook. The defenders do not, however. On the contrary, they welcome him as manna from Paris, because Onfray provides a vivid illustration of one of their central arguments. As Beale puts it, Onfray's vision is "the stark, rational articulation of that which the New Atheists do not dare to admit, either to themselves or to the reading public" (2008, 207). For the defenders, both Onfray the disciple and Nietzsche the master reveal a truth ignored by the rest of the New Atheists: atheism is "very costly – and very dangerous." "Contrary to modern atheists, who assure us that the death of God need not mean an end to morality, Nietzsche insisted that it did," argues D'Souza. "As God is the source of the moral law, His death means that the ground has been swept out from under us. We have become, in a sense, ethically groundless, and there is no more refuge to be taken in appeals to dignity and equality and compassion and all the rest. What confronts us, if we are honest, is the abyss" (2007, 268).

So Nietzsche said it. And Onfray repeated it. But are they *right*? Does atheism sweep all moral ground out from under us? Do we even have ground under us in the first place? That is, in the absence of atheism, could we rest secure upon firm ethical foundations? Chapter 6 will take up this question.

chapter six

The Defenders' Moral Foundations

In chapter 4 we examined the New Atheist claim that the most serious believers are the most dangerous, the most violent, the most intolerant. We did not critique the defenders' equivalent claim, that the only *logical* outcome of serious atheism is a nihilistic immorality. Those atheists who do not seem "shameless, that is, inhuman" (Crean 2007, 157) are those who have not worked out the full implications of their faulty metaphysics: they continue to live on ethical principles grounded in the very belief system they scorn. When an atheist arrives at consistency, then "the grinning skull of atheist post-nihilism" reveals itself (Beale 2008, 199).

This view rests on a crucial claim: a serious atheist has no good reasons to be ethical, because, once God is denied, ethical principles rest on *nothing*. For nearly all the defenders, *the* decisive difference between believers and atheists is that the former have good grounds for their morality, while the latter do not. This chapter will examine the theistic moral foundations presented by various defenders. While the chapter covers vital ground, its reach is limited: I will focus on works produced within the New Atheist debate, and I will argue that those defenders who claim to have identified a shared moral foundation are mistaken. This is not a trivial claim. Some very learned writers have weighed in thus far in the debate. Were there a convincing demonstration of the existence of a firm shared foundation out there somewhere, one would expect one of these learned writers to have referenced it in their own work. They have not done so.

I will understand a moral foundation to be a belief, or small set of interrelated beliefs, that constitutes a unified root for an entire system of morality. Such a foundation would have at least two dimensions: motivation and content. That is, a moral foundation would provide us with the desire to do right and avoid wrong, and with the means to distinguish the two.[1] In saying that a moral foundation would give us the desire to "do right and avoid wrong," it might be thought that I have prejudged an important issue, accepting the modern emphasis on morality as a set of rules, rather than an older ethical concern for who I am to *be*.[2] This is not so. The questions "what should I do?" and "who should I be?" cannot be divorced. To the critic who says we must not focus on rules to the neglect of "character" and "virtue," one might answer with Aristotle's insight that I can change who I am to *be* only by changing what I *do*: "By doing the acts that we do in our transactions with other men we become just or unjust, and by doing the acts that we do in the presence of danger, and being habituated to feel fear or confidence, we become brave or cowardly ... Thus, in one word, states of character arise out of like activities" (*Ethics* 1103b). So to be conscious of the question of the good life, of who I am to *be*, is simply to reflect on what I am to *do* in a broader, deeper way. To "do right and avoid wrong" is understood from a wider angle.[3]

The chapter will begin with an overview of the defenders' specific claims concerning moral foundations. We will then reflect on just what a shared foundation would look like, before arguing that none of the putative foundations put forth by the defenders clears the bar. I will show in particular that many of the critiques levelled by the defenders against the New Atheists' ethical claims apply equally well to the defenders' own claims.

1. The Defenders' Claims

While chapter 1 identified many deep differences among the defenders, on *this* there is near unanimity: when it comes to ethics, the believer has something that the unbeliever does not. On this point, liberals such as Ward or Haught sound much like conservatives such as Crean or Feser. Christian belief supplies the first dimension of a moral foundation: the motivation to do good. "The believer does what is right," declares Ward, " because the believer has been grasped by a vision of supreme personal goodness, by a glimpse of the vision of God" (2007, 137). Christian faith also looks after the second dimension: the actual content of morality. "The law of God," says Crean, is "a law written on our hearts and confirmed by revelation" (2007, 130). Wilson concurs: "A fixed standard, grounded in the character of God, allows us to define evil" (Hitchens and Wilson 2008, 66).

Atheists, on the other hand, lack any such foundation. They lack, first, *good reasons* to do good: "Whereas Christians and the faithful of other religions have rational reasons for attempting to live by their various moral systems," asserts Beale confidently, "the atheist does not" (2008, 262). Feser agrees: "An atheist or naturalist can *believe* in morality – that is a psychological fact – but he *cannot* have a *rational justification* for his belief – that is a philosophical fact" (2008, 221). Nor can atheism give any solid *content* to morality. Atheism, says Beale, "leaves every individual playing his own game and making up his own rules as he goes along" (2008, 190). The atheist, suggests Crean, is so devoid of moral guidance that he cannot even say that he has a duty "to educate his children rather than to torture them" (2007, 156). Even the more liberal Haught asks, "How can the atheist find a solid justification of ethical values?" (2008, 73).

The defenders allow that the individual atheist can be an ethical person, but only by being "a moral parasite, living his life on borrowed ethics" (Beale 2008, 263). The alternative to being a "moral parasite" is even worse. What happens when one consciously and deliberately ignores the content that only religion can supply to a sane moral system? For Beale the answer is obvious: "Nietzsche is the foremost example, but there is certainly no shortage of other individuals who do not fear to determine their own moral compass in the absence of God. We call them sociopaths and suicides" (2008, 266).

For Michael Novak, atheism operates as a time-release drug: "Widespread public atheism may not show its full effects right away, but only after three or four generations. For individual atheists 'of a peculiar character,' brought up in habits inculcated by the religious cultures of the past, can go on for two or three generations living in ways hard to distinguish from those of unassuming Christians and Jews" (2008, 52). Sooner or later, however, the borrowed ethics slacken their grip on us. One sees "a certain moral carelessness seeping into common life, a certain slacking off, a certain habit of getting away with things. Secularism may be livable among specially gifted people, but its effects on the general run of humankind seem to be less comforting" (268).[4]

One reason we cannot survive on "borrowed ethics" is that atheism can offer no rational objection to evil. Wilson asks: "When another atheist makes different ethical choices than you do (as Stalin and Mao certainly did), is there an overarching common standard for all atheists that you are obeying and which they are not obeying? If so, what is that standard and what book did it come from?" (Hitchens and Wilson 2008, 34). Moral decadence, says Novak, is a recurrent feature of human history, observed "ever since the fall of Rome." And he asks: "What tools does secularism possess to arrest such decadence? How does a secularist society even diagnose moral decadence? By whose standards?" (2008, 260).

To summarize the defenders' claims: religious belief provides us with both dimensions of a solid moral system. It teaches us what is right and what is wrong, and it provides us with the motivation to do what is right. Atheism can do neither. If the individual atheist does not seem to fulfil her destiny to be "shameless, that is, inhuman," as Crean so pithily puts it, that is only due to the vestigial effect of borrowed ethics. But this effect wears off over time. And then all hell breaks loose, so to speak.

2. Recognizing a "Moral Foundation"

Plato's Meno asked Socrates: "How will you look for something when you don't in the least know what it is? Even if you come right up against it, how will you know that what you have found is the thing you didn't know?" (80d). We seek a moral foundation:

how would we know were we to find it? Would it simply be something that I, personally, find adequate as a ground? Surely not: in such a case, almost anything could serve as a moral foundation. At the other extreme, would a moral foundation only be such if each and every last person acknowledged it? But that would raise the bar far too high: we would be demanding more of moral truth than of scientific truth. Perhaps the best formulation would be to say that, were we to "discover" it or find it in a book or "work it out" or "make it up," a moral foundation would be potentially recognizable as such to all reasonable people who have inquired diligently into the matter.[5]

And what might be the criteria for recognizing "reasonableness" or "diligence"? The key here is to avoid circularity. Thus, for example, it would be unacceptable to posit belief in God, or unbelief, as a criterion for reasonableness. This is precisely what Harris does. Such question-begging is also implicit in the arguments of many of the defenders, who simply place atheists outside the circle of those who are sane enough to recognize a moral foundation when they see it.

To avoid this, we must define reasonableness and a spirit of diligent inquiry in ways that do not exclude theists or atheists in advance. We might consider our everyday experiences of discussion: we can usually tell the difference between someone who is willing to explain their position and consider our own statements fairly, and someone who stubbornly refuses to enter into an honest and open discussion. Neither believers nor atheists have a monopoly on that sort of everyday reasonableness.

Given the marker I have suggested for a shared foundation: do the defenders provide us with one? They do not. I will first critique ethical claims advanced by particular defenders, and then show how arguments deployed against non-theistic ethical philosophies can be turned against the defenders' own ethical systems.

3. The Defenders' Foundations

Beale. We begin with Theodore Beale, who declares that "theists have a perfectly logical and objective basis for the application of their god-based moralities that even the most die-hard rational atheist cannot reject, given the theistic postulate that God actually exists and created the universe. In short, God's game, God's rules" (2008, 190). There is an obvious answer, offered centuries ago by Rousseau: "God himself has spoken: heed his revelation ... But to whom did he speak? He spoke to men. Why, then, did I hear nothing? He charged others to bring you his word. I understand: It is men who will tell me what God has said. I would have preferred to have heard God myself. It wouldn't have cost him anything more" (rpt. 1966, 387). In short, we have, not "God's rules" in some immediate sense, but a scriptural rendering of God's rules, a rendering which itself is interpreted in various ways by different people.

Nor does the difficulty end there. People with "itching ears," comments the second letter to Timothy, "will accumulate for themselves teachers to suit their own likings" (2 Tim 4:3). Unless I am scrupulously self-aware, the particular human beings to whom I turn for the interpretation of "God's rules" may well be chosen on the basis of my own "itching ears," to suit my own prior inclinations. This is hardly a firm foundation for a sensible believer, let alone for others.

Crean. We turn from the conservative fundamentalist Beale to the conservative Catholic Thomas Crean. Atheism, claims Crean, destroys the very "possibility of moral truth": morality must be "binding," and we can only be bound by a lawgiver "distinct from ourselves and from all human society," one who is in fact "law and wisdom itself" (2007, 99–104).[6] Let us observe Crean applying his own understanding of a morality grounded in God's "unchangeable nature." Seeking to counter Dawkins's claim that the God of the Old Testament is "the most unpleasant character in all fiction" (2006, 31), Crean tackles a gruesome verse from the book of Deuteronomy: "In the cities of these peoples that the Lord your God gives you for an inheritance, you shall save alive nothing that breathes" (Deut 20:16). Crean recognizes the implication that children are to be massacred along with everyone else, but does not find this troubling: "The lives they had from God could be justly ended by Him. Presumably, one reason why God ordained that this should be done was that in the absence of their parents, the children would have had no one to raise them. The souls of the infants would have survived death; and Catholic theologians hold that such souls enter a state of untroubled happiness, even if they do not enter heaven" (2007, 127).

Crean ignores, first, the same type of objection missed by Beale: Deuteronomy does not show us God ordering genocide, but rather human beings claiming that they have been ordered by God to commit genocide. But Crean goes further, offering a macabre appeal to sentimentality, as we are asked to imagine the fate of the poor orphans had God not solicitously ordered them wiped out along with their parents. This edifying example of "law and wisdom itself" at work is then completed with a repellent theological argument seeking to blunt our horror with the promise of "untroubled happiness" for the victims of this holy genocide. No shared foundation here.

Feser. Edward Feser is yet another conservative defender who offers a moral foundation, quite certain that no sane person could refuse the offer. Feser wishes to be systematic, building his foundation on the thought of Aristotle and Aquinas. For these two thinkers, Feser tells us, morality is "the habitual choice of actions that further the hierarchically ordered natural ends entailed by human nature" (2008, 122). And *why* should we choose such actions, why should we be moral in Feser's sense? For Feser, the matter is self-evident: when we understand that "the good for us is *in fact* whatever tends to fulfill our nature or essence in the sense of realizing the natural ends or purposes of our various natural capacities, then there can be no doubt as to why someone ought to do what is good in this sense" (137).

The *form* of Feser's argument closely resembles that of Sam Harris: both argue that once one accepts a point that to them is perfectly obvious, everything else follows of logical necessity. But while readers may feel that Harris's invocation of happiness is easy to understand, the implications of Feser's reliance on "the natural ends or purposes of our various natural capacities" are not immediately obvious. So Feser spells things out for us. The fact that we have an intellect, for example, means that "it is good for us – it fulfills our nature – to pursue truth and to avoid error" (2008, 137). It's unclear whether this would of itself persuade anyone to pursue or to tell the truth.[7] Consider now another natural capacity: the fact that we have sexual organs means ... what, exactly? It is obvious, argues Feser, that the purpose of sex is procreation, and that pleasure is simply a means of getting people to pursue that purpose (141–2).[8] Now "sexual arousal is hard to resist," comments Feser, and *that* shows that "Mother Nature" wants us to have "lots" of babies (142–3). Given the state of the planet at the moment, many of us will be inclined to ignore the alleged views of "Mother Nature" on this matter. But that, says Feser, we must not do. The point of sex being procreation, "the man and the woman involved in such an act cannot act in a way to prevent this result" (146).

The reader will recognize that Feser's position parallels that of the Vatican. This alignment should provoke some doubt as to whether Feser's framework offers a plausible *shared* foundation for morality. The Vatican's arguments on contraception, after all, have proven manifestly unpersuasive among Catholics themselves, let alone citizens in general.[9] This does not show that Feser's individual moral judgments are incorrect: such judgments cannot be evaluated by opinion polls. Feser might argue that the lack of agreement with his type of argument is itself a symptom of fallenness, of moral degeneration, a response that also parallels the Vatican position (Pius XII, *Humani Generis*, para. 2). Even were this true, we would still be left with the question of how to deal with this fallenness. In any event, the argument that Christian belief provides a shared foundation for morality is obviously weakened when one's specific moral claims are rejected by most Christians.

Haught. Let us now consider the foundationalist claims of a liberal theologian: John Haught. Haught does not attempt to provide a religious justification for the current moral concerns of American conservatives. Nor is he committed to biblical literalism. Not surprisingly, then, Haught is rebuked by one of the conservative defenders for his "accommodationist response to the New Atheism" (Mohler 2008, 102). Despite his liberal theology, however, Haught is a moral foundationalist: "Faith is what gives reason a future, and morality a meaning" (2008, 75). The New Atheists, argues Haught, avoid the question of "how to justify our moral precepts so that we are bound by them unconditionally" (73). Believers need not avoid the matter: the "theological understanding of reality," claims Haught, "can elegantly justify both the trust we have in our minds and the sense of rightness that stands behind our moral protest" (74).

Haught's particular "theological understanding of reality" might possibly supply some people with one of the dimensions of a moral foundation, the motivation to do good, though its degree of abstraction sparks doubt on this score.[10] The other dimension of a moral foundation, *content*, is manifestly neglected by Haught. "We can trust our sense of outrage at evil," argues Haught, "ultimately because we are already grasped by a goodness that is not made by ourselves, or by our genes, but which is the silent and unobtrusive goal of all our moral striving" (2008, 75). But how do we know that our outrage in this or that *specific case* is truly grounded in a "goodness that is not made by ourselves"? Haught argues that our belief in God gives grounding to moral judgment in principle, but does it support any *concrete* moral judgments? That is certainly a crucial question, a question on which Haught is silent.

In summary: whether we consider conservative defenders such as Beale, Crean, or Feser, or a liberal defender such as Haught, we find their foundationalist claims falling before quite reasonable and even obvious objections. As we will now see, many of the defenders' critiques of atheists' supposedly arbitrary morality also undermine their own foundationalist claims.

4. Rebounding Critiques

Philosopher of science Karl Popper offered the reasonable suggestion that "after having produced some criticism of a rival theory, we should always make a serious attempt to apply this or a similar criticism to our own theory" (2002, 65). In presenting their foundationalist claims, and their critiques of atheist morality, the defenders have ignored Popper's advice.

Absolutely binding morality? Crean observes that "morality is by definition something *binding*" (2007, 99). Haught also holds that we must seek to "justify our moral precepts so that we are bound by them unconditionally" (2008, 73). The defenders generally argue that the New Atheists fail to present a moral code that is even remotely binding.

The defenders are right to emphasize the binding quality of morality. We experience a moral injunction as a *demand* upon us, and thus as quite distinct from a mere "preference" that we happen to espouse. At the same time, it should be obvious that neither believers nor unbelievers consistently act as if we were "unconditionally" bound by moral rules. One might say that the person of "absolute" faith would live out an absolutely binding morality, and in that sense faith provides a firm foundation for morality. But could one not say the same for the person whose "love of humanity" was absolute? We know, of course, that individuals of either type are rare, if they exist at all.

In practice, believers over the millennia have recognized that individual faith is not sufficient to generate a binding morality: this is precisely why they have tried to structure societies and institutions in order to reduce temptations to "go astray." The Catholic Church's Index of prohibited books, or the efforts by Christian conservatives to keep topics they consider immoral out of public classrooms, to say nothing of the persecution of heretics and alleged witches, all reflect an understanding that individual faith alone is insufficient protection against the snares of the "Evil One."

We must not raise and lower the bar as we evaluate different approaches to morality: if we observe secular moral systems with a cold-eyed sociological realism, then we must do the same for moral systems rooted in Christianity. In all cases, we will observe a disjunction between the *experience* of morality as something binding and the actual *practice* of fallible human beings.

Who says? In their 2007 debate, Douglas Wilson aimed a series of questions at Christopher Hitchens's all-too-casual claim that binding ethical rules are "derived from innate human solidarity": "Derived by whom? Is this derivation authoritative? Do the rest of us ever get to vote on which derivations represent true, innate human solidarity? Do we ever get to vote on the authorized derivers? On what basis is innate human solidarity authoritative? ... Are there different denominations that read the book of innate

human solidarity differently? Which one is right? Who says?"
(Hitchens and Wilson 2008, 41).

Is there a single one of these questions that cannot be turned
around and aimed at a Christian foundationalist? Consider the
claim that our shared ethical rules can be derived from a biblical
foundation: each of Wilson's questions, suitably modified, applies.
Do the rest of us ever get to vote on which derivations represent
true, biblical morality? Are there different denominations that read
the Bible differently? Which one is right? Who says?

What about people who ...? Feser critiques philosopher John
Rawls's attempt to develop a secular system of ethics. Rawls, says
Feser, assumes that subjects recognize each other's equal "moral
worth," which leads Feser to ask, "But what justifies the key pre-
sumption that people *really have* moral worth in the first place? ...
And the answer seems always to be just to repeat that these are
'intuitions' we all have, or at least that all decent people have."
And that naturally leads to what I will call the "Feser-question":
"And what about people who don't share these intuitions? Well,
you know, we'd just better make sure such people don't win out"
(2008, 219).

Feser's representation of Rawls is problematic.[11] That aside, note
the rebounding nature of his critique. We can certainly ask of Feser:
"And what about people you cannot persuade of the rightness of
your own natural law ethics?" Feser would have to answer that he
hopes they "don't win out." More precisely, Feser appears to have
abandoned that hope, believing that the evil ones have *already*
won. He is thus reduced to lamenting "the extreme depravity into
which modern civilization has fallen" (2008, 151).

In fact, theistic foundations may be *more* vulnerable to the Feser-
question than others. Defender Paul Copan argues that moral theories such as those of Kant or John Rawls *presuppose* "human
dignity and personal responsibility," but they cannot provide a
"decent metaphysical account" of them (2008, 151). But just when
does one need an "account" of a central good such as human dignity? Only when it is called into question. Now in the face of someone who radically questions the very idea of human dignity, it is
true that the ethical theories of Kant or Rawls don't have much to

say. But what theory does? Can anyone honestly claim that referring to God will provide much support in such a situation? Even the Bible suggests otherwise: "He who does not love his brother whom he has seen, cannot love God whom he has not seen" (1 Jn 4:20). Someone who does not understand the value of human dignity is simply "vicious." Faced with such a person, it is pointless to cast about for alternative foundations, because no foundation is foundational to the person who rejects it. Instead, we must search for ethical "footholds," points of contact between their lives and the ethical value we are trying to defend. That is, if we are to have any hope of bringing such a person back to humanity, we must appeal to things they already know, to sentiments, to memories. In this way, we may be able to reawaken a sense of human dignity. While this path may fail, it offers more hope than trying to persuade them by way of arguments based upon a God with whom they have radically lost contact.

5. Conclusion

A key claim unites otherwise disparate defenders: *we* have a foundation for morality, hence *our* ethics are rational, and *theirs* are not. But when we examined the foundationalist arguments advanced by a cross-section of defenders, we found that their arguments could not survive critical scrutiny. Moreover, we saw that the critiques the defenders level against the viability of atheist morality can sink their own moral claims.

We must now examine just how societies survive without such foundations, and the moral tasks that we must confront in light of our foundationless condition.

chapter seven

Can We Live without Foundations?

The previous two chapters have shown that those parties to the New Atheist debate who claim to have identified a shared moral foundation are mistaken. I will jump from that finding to a general claim, which I simply stipulate: we must find our way in this world without shared moral foundations. The claim is *intrinsically* unprovable.[1] It is, however, falsifiable. But how? It is obviously not enough to point to an author or argument that one finds persuasive. One must demonstrate that one's candidate for a moral foundation could appeal to people holding a wide range of metaphysical outlooks. So let a set of sophisticated and thoughtful atheists, agnostics, and believers of various types come together and discuss the merits and shortcomings of any putative ethical foundation. And then invite yet others to subject that possible foundation to critical scrutiny. And when it has survived those tests, then and only then can we have some confidence that a shared foundation has been found. And perhaps we will be right. Or perhaps another generation will come along and demonstrate that those who scrutinized our foundation, diverse and thoughtful though they were, nevertheless failed to detect important weaknesses.

Meeting this challenge is the only *serious* way to refute the general claim stipulated here. There is, however, an *illegitimate* way to bypass the claim: the expulsion of certain categories of people from the "we" that must seek ethical consensus. Indeed, the frustrated quest for shared foundations creates a strong temptation for such exclusion, as we will see.

1. Foundationalism's Risks

A shared moral foundation is not available. Moreover, the contrary view has its risks. Foundationalist claims can drive one to nihilism, in two easy steps. One first accepts an argument that this or that is the only available foundation for morality, and that, without it, chaos reigns. The second step occurs when one realizes that the trusted foundation is not in fact solid.

Some claims in the New Atheist debate can lead the unwary reader to take the first step. David Berlinski argues that "if moral imperatives are not commanded by God's will, and if they are not in some sense absolute, then what ought to be is a matter simply of what men and women decide should be. There is no other source of judgment. What is this if not another way of saying that *if God does not exist, everything is permitted*?" (2008, 40). One may not be impressed by the logic of Berlinski's argument,[2] but the endpoint is clear enough: to give up God is to give up the possibility of morality itself. Feser likewise does unwitting service to nihilism. "If 'same-sex marriage' is not contrary to nature," he fulminates, "then nothing is; and if nothing is contrary to nature, then (as we will see) there can be no grounds whatsoever for moral judgment" (2008, 150). Given the "extreme depravity" of our time, Feser sees himself as a prophet-in-despair, hurling shrill anathemas at the modern world, which seduces us with "lots of neat-o-gizmos with which to while away our pointless lives now that purpose has been utterly banished from the world by naturalistic diktat" (2008, 178). Sam Harris also gets into the act: after attempting to develop a rather confused consequentialist ethics, he comments: "The fact that it may often be difficult, or even impossible, to know what the consequences of our thoughts and actions will be does not mean that there is some other basis for human values that is worth worrying about" (2010, 72).

For others, foundationalism does not lead to nihilism as such, but to something closely related: a complete subjectivization of ethics. Thus, "the complete impossibility of finding any arguments to prove that this or that has intrinsic value" leads Bertrand Russell to argue for the "subjectivity of values." Arguments over values, he suggests, are as futile as arguments about personal tastes: "If one man says 'oysters are good' and another says 'I think they are bad,' we recognize that there is nothing to argue about" (rpt. 1997, 237–8). So too with normative discussions. This outlook is much more influential today than outright nihilism. It is drilled into many economics students at the outset of their studies,[3] and is a staple of the research-methods textbooks inflicted on social science students. We enjoy, it is claimed, some body of objective, firmly grounded, scientific knowledge. "Values" aren't like that at all, and so they are purely subjective.

Neither nihilism nor pure subjectivism, however, are psychologically comfortable states of affairs. "Man is not naturally a doubting animal," as Gilson comments (1937, 120). And this suggests a major *temptation* for some Christians. Consider a hypothetical response to the critiques offered in the previous chapter: "You have made good arguments about the problem of foundations, but these arguments only hold in a deeply *pluralist* society. We are not such a society: we are, in our vast majority, a Christian people. We are the majority, and in a democracy, the majority rules. So let's have *Christian* moral foundations for a *Christian* people." One might respond that it is *unchristian* to assert that our shared ethics must have a Christian foundation. I would not be happy to be forced to obey a law whose only justification was its presence in the Koran. And so, if I expect non-Christians to submit to a law whose only justification is biblical, I betray the biblical command to treat others as we wish to be treated. A certain type of Christian would have an answer to this argument:

> Your analogy fails, because the Bible is *true*, and the Koran is not. So while it is unjust to force people to live according to the Koran, it is not unjust to force a biblical ethics upon them. In fact, such force is in the unbeliever's *true*, eternal, interest. There is, after all, a chance that the unbeliever will eventually come to obey for the right reasons the morality that she is at first forced to obey. In any case, even if we fail to save this or that unbeliever through our theocracy (for that is what is being proposed, if we are honest), at least we can prevent the unbeliever from infecting others.

Is this answer improbably extreme? Consider defender Albert Mohler's assertion that any belief system "that keeps persons captive and keeps them from coming to faith in the Lord Jesus Christ, yes, is a demonstration of satanic power" (qtd. in Roach 2006). Mohler offered Islam, Buddhism, Hinduism, and "dialectical materialism" as examples of satanic power. Given this outlook, it would not make a lot of sense to fret over trampling on the religious sensibilities of non-Christian citizens, as those sensibilities are merely a tragic symptom of their "captivity" to Satan.[4]

In the end, non-Christian beliefs would not be the only ones trampled underfoot. Chapter 4 examined the history of Christians' usage of scripture. This history, and the deep ethical differences between the current defenders, demonstrate that one *cannot* derive a reasonably complete ethical system from Christianity as such, but only from this or that particular interpretation of Christianity. Only someone who believes that their particular interpretation is the one and only true one can assert that there is *a* Christian position on most political and ethical issues.

I have been discussing a *temptation*, not a state of affairs I consider likely to come about any time soon. Still, in various countries in the last century, authoritarian regimes emerged in a context of general "fatigue" with democracy. Frustration with our lack of shared moral foundations, and a belief that such foundations might be attainable if pluralism were curtailed, might certainly contribute to such fatigue. Apart from this admittedly speculative possibility, I have argued that foundationalism is demonstrably risky. The danger arises from thinking that unless we have a shared and unshakable ethical foundation we have nothing, and morality becomes a matter of subjective whim. The danger lies in forgetting that somehow we make our way through the world with beliefs, factual and ethical, of which we are *more or less* subjectively certain, which are *more or less* widely shared by others, which are *more or less* able to withstand critical scrutiny.

2. How Do We Manage?

But how exactly do we do this? How, if modern societies do not have shared moral foundations, do they survive? Why do they not descend into chaos? Let us examine for a moment just one of the aspects of a moral foundation, the dimension of motivation. That is, let us consider why people respect norms, without asking, for now, just where those norms come from.[5] Though the following list is not exhaustive, and does not attempt to capture all the nuances in our motives, it will serve to indicate how we get along without foundations.[6]

We should note, first, that much behaviour is not directly "motivated" at all, it is simply habitual. Norms often influence behaviour via habit, with no conscious decision to follow those norms. Because the outcome of conscious consideration is uncertain, many have argued that only habitual respect can stabilize a social institution. "It is from habit, and only from habit," held Aristotle, "that law derives the validity which secures obedience" (*Politics* 1269a).

But habits must be formed in the first place. And they can be challenged, even by other habits. So let us consider various motivations. We are all affected by fear of some form of punishment or disapproval: from parents, first in life, from other authority figures, from friends and one's peer groups, from employers or the state. Some forms of this influence are quite heavy-handed: for example, the public torture and execution depicted by Foucault at the outset of his *Surveiller et punir* (1975). Other forms are quite subtle: we are influenced by frowns and raised eyebrows, by a certain hesitancy in the way another responds to our suggestion, and so on.

The counterpart of fear is the desire for approval and reward. The approval of others is intimately linked to another powerful motivation, related to our self-understanding.[7] This motive can lead to smug self-satisfaction. In Camus's *La chute*, Jean-Baptiste Clamence seeks occasions to do good in order to heighten his *enjoyment* of himself as a doer of good (1956, 24–5).[8] But the concern for one's self-understanding can operate in a very different mode, reflecting a simple desire to be at peace with oneself. In Plato's *Hippias Major*, Socrates says that upon returning home he has to give an account of himself to a "constant inquisitor of mine – constant, because he happens to be a very close relative and to share the same house" (304d). Interpreters take this "very close relative" to be Socrates himself. For Hannah Arendt, Socrates's statement is central to his way of life: "Better to be at odds with the whole world than be at odds with the only one you are forced to live together with when you have left company behind" (1978, 188).

Another motivation is linked to particular relationships. One does something simply because one believes that this is what someone in such a relation must do. A parent stays up with a sick child; a friend listens to a friend pour out her anguish. The concern for self-image, in either of its modes, doesn't enter in here: one simply does what one feels one must. There is a self-forgetfulness, nicely captured by the Gospel injunction not to let the left hand know what the right hand is doing.[9] The love enacted in such relationships may function as a school of responsibility, helping to form "human selves who find concern for others entirely natural" (Rorty 1999, 78). Apart from the love arising from personal relations, many people are also shaped by broader loves: of God; of humanity; of the natural world; of justice.[10]

In practice, these various motives often work together. Concern to perform well at work, for example, may be motivated by a desire for rewards of various sorts, by a concern for self-respect, and by an unselfconscious sense of responsibility. We may not even be able to disentangle our own motives. This entanglement of motives, Adam Smith noted, led some "splenetic philosophers" to reduce the desire to do right to mere vanity (2009, 151), just as some modern thinkers use "psychic income" as an all-purpose explanation to rule out disinterested behaviour (Becker 1981, 11).

3. Do Motives Have Foundations?

None of the motives just examined depend on clear foundations. In the face of social disapproval, for example, we do not normally inquire into the ultimate foundations of the judgment. Usually the desire for the approval of others requires no more support than the fact that, generally speaking, it is more pleasant to get along with people than otherwise. We do, of course, question particular judgments. Depending on context, our question may or may not receive an answer. Even if it does, the answer will certainly be one that could be queried in its turn. Such a process will end long before it has reached some bedrock justification for the approval or disapproval.

Thus, in practice we respect norms for "non-foundational" reasons. To this a foundationalist may well reply:

> That's all very fine when things are going well, but not otherwise. How do all your "non-foundational" motives answer a radical challenge to morality? Social disapproval? But what of the person who has learned how "to seem to be just when one is not" (*Republic* 361a)? Are we to appeal to their conscience? What if they give us the answer of *The Tempest*'s Antonio: "I feel not this deity in my bosom"?

The questions are valid. But in the face of radical challenge, how exactly do foundations help us? There are *always* answers to brush away someone's preferred moral foundation, should the radical critic be determined to do so.

Thus, one person might seek to ground ethics in the Kantian principle that action is ethical if it reflects a maxim of conduct that one can will to become universal (rpt. 1964, para. 52–5). She might seek to reason with the radical critic on that basis, but this will only work if the critic accepts the reasoning process itself. Suppose she puts to the critic the Kantian question we often ask children when trying to explain why a certain action is wrong: "What if everyone did that?" It's a useful question, but the critic may simply brush it aside.[11]

Another person appeals to a divine foundation. Should the appeal invoke the biblical God in particular, the critic might well mention the inconvenient story of the Amalekites, and the even more inconvenient use of that story by the early American colonists. The critic might then ask: so if your God orders genocide, just what does he rule out, exactly? And if your God has truly declared that only Christians can be saved, as many of you folks believe, and that those who happen not to have been born in a Christian society are barred from heaven, why should I be interested in the moral views of that "most unjust and cruel of tyrants" (Rousseau rpt. 1966, 387)?

The last two sections should not be read as a declaration of optimism. I have argued that societies get along without shared foundations. I have not claimed that they get on *particularly well*. All the motives for normative behaviour considered above, and others that may have occurred to the reader, have been in force throughout the great catastrophes of history, as they are today, and as they will be during the catastrophes of the future. But if these motives can coexist with widespread evil, it is not because they lack foundations. The problem lies elsewhere.

4. A Tangle of Norms

We have discussed motivations to respect norms without any consideration of the content of those norms. Let us now consider the range of norms to which a modern individual is subject, norms that enter into myriad contradictions with one another. It is helpful first to ask from whence norms come. The New Atheist debate has focused on norms linked to religious belief, or to a conscious "secular humanism," but these are only part of a complex picture. Nicholas Wolterstorff comments: "Requirements come from many sources: from the laws of the land in which one lives, from the rules of the game one is playing, from the rules of politeness in one's society, from the rules of etiquette for a person of one's status, from one or another social role that one fills, and ... from some command issued to one" (2008, 277).

If we unpack each element in Wolterstorff's list, we can see that already a wide range of demands is involved. We occupy various social roles, for example, and we can occupy more than one role at the same time. Yet there are also expectations that Wolterstorff's list doesn't quite capture. In much of life, for example, there is an expectation not simply that we *play* by the rules, but that we *win*. Bellah et al. note that "American individualism ... adulates winners while showing contempt for losers, a contempt that can descend with crushing weight on those considered, either by others or by themselves, to be moral or social failures" (2008, xiv). Their reference to *moral* failure highlights how expectations that upon reflection would appear unconnected to the moral sphere can in practice take on a moral colouring for those subject to them. Social approval and disapproval are in no way limited to enforcement of some recognizable and defensible moral code. Consider Smith's observation: "The fortunate and the proud wonder at the insolence of human wretchedness, that it should dare to present itself before them, and with the loathsome aspect of its misery presume to disturb the serenity of their happiness" (2009, 64). He could well be talking of modern-day reactions to the homeless and to panhandlers: economic failure is condemned as *bad taste*, which is to kept hidden away.[12]

There are other normative expectations linked to winning. One concerns the ability and willingness to stand up for oneself. The Christian ethic of forgiveness has always coexisted with this opposed norm: "A person becomes contemptible who tamely sits still, and submits to insults, without attempting either to repel or to revenge them" (Smith 2009, 43). When Shakespeare's King Richard II calls on Bolingbroke to back down from his quarrel with Mowbray, Bolingbroke exclaims, "O, God defend my soul from such deep sin!" (1.1).

One may object that the "ethic" of success obliterates the vital distinction between specifically *moral* obligation and other types of demands upon people. It certainly does, but we are examining here the range of norms that generate demands that many people experience, rightly or wrongly, as obligatory. And the ethic of success is a fertile source of such demands.

Apart from all these demands that come from "outside" us, there are normative expectations that, in a sense, the self places upon itself, though society is often the source of these demands, at one remove. One such demand is "to thine own self be true" (*Hamlet*, 1.3). For Charles Taylor, this demand is so influential today that we can be said to be living in "The age of authenticity" (2007, 473f.), exemplified in Abraham Maslow's enthroning of "self-actualization" as the *highest* human need: "What a man can be, he must be" (rpt. 1987, 142).

When one considers the wide range of demands put upon us, the demands of our social roles, the manipulative pressures of advertising, the myriad social pressures to conform to an image of decency and success, and so on, it is clear that we're not free agents who have to be persuaded that the word *ought* means something. We're social beings nearly drowning in an endless welter of oughts and musts. Even many of what we think of as our deeply personal desires and goals have been shaped by that chaotic welter of demands upon us. We are not, obviously, subject only to normative demands for which we can identify a satisfactory foundation. We are "always already" immersed in norms. The main challenge we must face is not to ground our "oughts" in a foundation, because there really is no escaping from them: the rejection of *some* demands will increase our subjection to others.

These considerations show that there is something profoundly unrealistic in the New Atheist debate's treatment of ethical matters. The debate floats along above the social world, creating a mythical space in which believers and unbelievers joust for supremacy, both sides imagining that everything hinges on the outcome of their battle, both sides resolutely ignoring the wide range of normative demands upon people, demands for the most part entirely unhinged from metaphysical matters.

We are born into a world of *oughts* and *musts* in which we must find our way.[13] And it is a profoundly contradictory world. The contradictions between the desires and behaviour that advertisers seek to encourage in us and the injunctions of many moral codes are fairly obvious. So too is the tension between the range of moral injunctions concerning how to play the various games of life, and the imperative to succeed in those games. There are also important contradictions between various social roles we may occupy. Consider the corporate manager who accepts Milton Friedman's argument that it is "intolerable" to "make expenditures on reducing pollution beyond the amount that is in the best interests of the corporation or that is required by law" (1970). He will feel *morally obligated* to perform actions that are repugnant to him in his role of responsible neighbour and citizen. These are not the sorts of contradictions upon which much polemic tends to focus: between the beliefs of liberals and conservatives, for example, or between those of believers of various types, agnostics, and atheists.

5. The Citizen as Moral Theorist

After listing the range of demands upon us, Wolterstorff comments that "one of the tasks of the moral theorist is to determine where, in this panoply of requirements, *moral* requirements are to be found" (2008, 277). But in this respect must we not all be moral theorists? Are we not all faced with the challenge, not simply of distinguishing what we *wish* to do and be from what we *ought* to do and be, but also to recognize, among all the *oughts* that confront us, those oughts that we really ought to heed?[14]

I have argued that we do not have *shared* foundations. But do individuals, at least, rely on a firm foundation in order to sort out the moral demands they face? Perhaps, though that foundation is likely to be far more complex, and in a sense much less foundational, than the unreflective individual might think. One person might take as a starting point for ethical reflection, for example, a conception of the biblical God. But that conception will draw on much else. God may be sovereign over the universe, but our *conception* of God is not sovereign over our other beliefs. As William James pointed out a century ago:

> Nothing is more striking than the secular alteration that goes on in the moral and religious tone of men, as their insight into nature and their social arrangements progressively develop. After an interval of a few generations the mental climate proves unfavorable to notions of the deity which at an earlier date were perfectly satisfactory ... What with science, idealism, and democracy, our own imagination has grown to need a God of an entirely different temperament from that Being interested exclusively in dealing out personal favors, with whom our ancestors were so contented. Smitten as we are with the vision of social righteousness, a God indifferent to everything but adulation, and full of partiality

for his individual favorites, lacks an essential element of largeness. (rpt. 1999, 360, 378)

One might condemn this as an unacceptable subordination of biblical revelation to the spirit of each age, were it not clear that understandings of God develop throughout the Bible itself: an evolving understanding of God is faithful to the Bible.

A certain type of believer will recoil in horror at this: God is lord of the universe, she will argue, and we have no business subjecting the word of God to the whimsical judgment of our age. If we allow our morality to be influenced by the world around us, we will end up "cherry-picking" from the Bible.[15] We can answer by noting that all of us set great store by the evidence of our own eyes, yet all of us believe that the earth orbits the sun, though our eyes tell us otherwise. Are we "cherry-picking" the evidence of our senses? Clearly, we are interpreting that evidence in light of other sources of knowledge. Analogously, believers have always interpreted the Bible in light of other sources of moral knowledge, and interpreted specific *parts* of the Bible in light of their evolving understanding of the *whole*.

We might draw a distinction between two broad ways of seeking to ground one's life and morality in a particular good. One individual is open to all manner of insights in trying to deepen her understanding of that good. She has committed herself, but does not fully understand to what (or, as the case may be, to *whom*). Understanding unfolds in living the commitment over time. A very different person thinks at the outset that he already fully understands his foundational good, and proceeds to "deduce" the consequences for practice.

Among the dangers of the latter approach is that of losing openness to the individual situation. A moving passage in Chinua Achebe's *Things Fall Apart* recounts how young Nwoye heard "the voice of an infant crying in the thick forest." It was, he realized, the cry of a twin, victim of a custom in which "twins were put in earthenware pots and thrown away in the forest." Nwoye felt "a snapping inside him," a gut reaction that would eventually lead him to turn his back on much of his inherited culture (1959, 60). The story is striking. Twin infanticide, it seems, was culturally approved, but his visceral reaction shows that Nwoye was more than a pure child of his culture. One can ask: why should one heed such a gut reaction? One good reason is that it demands to be heeded. It is not a timid, tentative suggestion. As our label for it suggests, it is much more *visceral* and forceful. This does not mean that our gut reactions are infallible. They are a form of "moral data," to be tested by reason and weighed against our existing morality, but which also put our reasoning and existing morality to the test. As we saw when considering Harris's justification for the torture of innocent people, spontaneous revulsion may be an important alarm bell that prevents us from imputing infallibility to a dubious chain of moral reasoning. These reactions are most powerfully triggered, not by abstractions, but by concrete cases. It would seem vital, then, that one's individual moral foundation, whatever its source, remain "permeable" to insights arising from concrete situations, as the individual foundation and the morality built upon it are fallible.

6. The Fabric of Belief

I have suggested that we don't sort out the demands upon us on the basis of some simple foundation. How then do we proceed? To answer, I will draw upon insights from the philosophy of science. And what have science and ethics to do with one another? It is certainly a mistake to take some image of scientific method and apply it to other areas of knowledge, all the more so because such images are often simplistic. But it is certainly *not* a mistake to take into account what has been learned through reflection on science concerning the general limits and problems of human knowledge. Doing so will turn up some surprising parallels. Charles Taylor argues, for example, that "scientific revolutions" share an important feature with moral disputes: both are rendered insoluble by the "erroneous model of foundationalist reasoning" (1995, 49), a claim clearly relevant to the matter at hand.

W.V. Quine presents a striking image: the totality of our beliefs form a "man-made fabric which impinges on experience only along the edges." Any "conflict with experience at the periphery occasions readjustments in the interior of the field." But the whole fabric is "undetermined" by experience, hence we have a lot of scope in making such adjustments (1951, 39). In those adjustments, we manifest a "natural tendency to disturb the total system as little as possible" (41).

As the metaphor suggests, there is no foundation to this "fabric." Observed facts do not constitute a ground floor for objective knowledge. An otherwise divided set of philosophers of science are united on this one point: what we observe, we observe with the guidance of our explicit and implicit theories (Popper 2002, 37; Kuhn 1970, 7; Lakatos 1970, 99). Theories are brought before the bar of observation and experience, but the latter are also put to the test by theories. Observations that cannot be accounted for within any existing theoretical framework will generally be treated as suspect, rather than serving to falsify existing theories.

Further, the fabric is not fully transparent. Paul Feyerabend notes, for example, that "Einstein's analysis of simultaneity unearthed some features of the Newtonian cosmology which, though unknown, had influenced all arguments about space and time" (1993, 166). Just as a scientific theory can rely on assumptions that are not fully understood, so too does it have implications that only come to be identified over time. An eventually powerful challenge to the Newtonian system was a minute anomaly in the perihelion of Mercury. It took quite some time in the development of the Newtonian paradigm to recognize that it even *had* clear implications for the perihelion.

Let us apply these notions to everyday life. They are relevant, first, to the alleged gulf between "facts" and "values." In practice, we can assume that every "normative" proposition is linked to implicit or explicit fact claims.[16] This link will be conscious for some people, but not for others. Thus, my views on capital punishment may simply be absorbed from my milieu, and it is only when challenged that I begin to identify some of the factual supports for those views. These supporting propositions also have their supporting propositions.[17] And as in the case of scientific theories, there's no reason to believe that all these supports refer back to a firm foundation. Aristotle's observation that "it is impossible to prove everything, for then there would arise an infinite regression" (*Metaphysics*, 1006a) holds for both factual and normative beliefs.

As with science, the fabric of our everyday beliefs is not fully transparent to us. The supporter of capital punishment, for example, likely assumes that the probability of a wrongful execution is infinitesimally low, a belief that in turn rests on a host of unarticulated beliefs about the nature of society. But unlike tacit scientific beliefs about the concept of simultaneity, many of our everyday beliefs can affect the way we live our lives. This adds another sort of non-transparency, in that we are not always certain exactly *how firmly* we hold particular beliefs. C.S. Lewis illustrates this with a vivid example (1977, 121). A child is learning to swim. His belief that he can float is only one factor influencing his behaviour once he is released in the water. The knowledge that all sorts of things sink in water is also present in his mind. So too is the survival instinct that wordlessly warns him not to attempt so foolish a thing as to float. His response to being released in the water will reflect the outcome of a contest between these various influences, an outcome *not known in advance*. In the same way, we cannot be certain in advance just how our ethical beliefs will fare in particularly difficult situations.

Just as the implications of a scientific theory are not all clear to its original formulators, an everyday belief can also have a set of implications, a set of unknown magnitude. A particular belief may over time have consequences for the way we live and. see the world, of which we are entirely unaware when we first embrace the belief. This can happen at an individual level. The unforeseen implications of beliefs can emerge at a social level as well. Summing up the paradoxical fate of the Christian Reformation, initially so hostile to emerging capitalism yet eventually so congenial to it, historian R.H. Tawney likened the "children of the mind" to those of the body: "If their parents could foresee their future development, it would sometimes break their hearts" (1954, 81).

I have noted various parallels between scientific theories and everyday beliefs, as well as the important difference that the latter, as they shape our actions, may be believed only to a certain degree. There is another crucial difference between the scientific and the everyday. Whereas science evolves by both generating and addressing contradictions in its system of beliefs (Kuhn 1970, 65), the fabric of our everyday beliefs is more loosely knit, allowing for contradictions and much vagueness. These contradictions are often revealing: they are "permitted contradictions," those that have not been brought forcefully to our attention one way or another, or that we have allowed ourselves to continue affirming, even after becoming aware of them. In many cases such contradictions are "functional," allowing us to sustain our often-contradictory practices.

7. Implications of the Fabric

Richard Rorty once suggested that "in political discussion with those outside the relevant religious community, [religion] is a conversation-stopper" (1999, 171). It is odd that he should have singled out religion in this regard: when it comes to political or ethical issues, our culture is littered with conversation stoppers.[18] One of the most potent of these, wedded to a surprising variety of outlooks, might be termed "foundational pessimism." This holds that if we push a normative discussion far enough, we reach a bedrock of "fundamental differences in basic values, differences about which men can ultimately only fight," as Milton Friedman put it (1953, 5). Concurring with the economist Friedman, we have: the positivist philosopher A.J. Ayer, who suggests that in a discussion over values "we finally resort to mere abuse" (1946, 111); the sociologist Max Weber, who likens conflicting orientations in basic life values to an "unceasing struggle of ... gods with one another" (1958, 152); and philosopher Alasdair MacIntyre, who views modern moral debates as "interminable" because of the "conceptual incommensurability" of rival positions (1984, 6, 8).

MacIntyre, Friedman, Ayer, Weber: what diverse thinkers arrive at the same conclusion. And must one not draw from their argument the practical conclusion that normative dialogue is a pointless exercise? Why embark on an attempt at mutual understanding that can never result in understanding? If taken seriously, foundational pessimism would be *worse* than a conversation stopper: it would prevent conversations from even starting.

But if we recognize that our beliefs form a fabric, that normative and empirical claims are intertwined, and that this fabric need not have a foundation, *there is always something we can talk about.* We need never reach a final impasse. We may, of course, turn away from dialogue, or simply run out of energy, but that is another question.[19]

But does not a believer's appeal to "God's will" bring dialogue to the end of the line? Is it not, as Rorty claimed, a conversation-stopper? Not at all. For someone to say "I believe we must do X because God calls on us to do it" would not be the *end* of the discussion, but simply another claim up for debate. One might ask: Just what are your grounds for believing that God calls us to this? If the answer referred to this or that biblical verse, a number of follow-up questions would suggest themselves: But is this particular biblical call, as you understand it, consistent with the central thrust of the biblical message? What do you understand that central thrust to be, and what are your grounds for thinking that? After all, as we saw in chapter 4, the fact that a statement appears in the Bible is not sufficient grounds for it to be taken as ethically binding. Once it is understood that "The Bible says ..." is not a conversation stopper, the claim that a particular biblical command must be followed today becomes a normative claim like any other, amenable to rational discussion.

A further implication of the fabric of beliefs is that a "foundationalist gambit" is not a helpful conversational move. In the Wilson-Hitchens encounter, Wilson repeatedly suggests that Hitchens's atheism leaves his moral claims, including those concerning religion, without support:

> Your book and your installments in this debate thus far are filled with fierce denunciations of various manifestations of immorality. You are playing Savonarola here, and I simply want to know the basis of your florid denunciations. You preach like some hot gospeler – with a floppy

leather-bound book and all. I know the book is not the Bible and so all I want to know is what book it is, and why it has anything to do with me. Why should anyone listen to your jeremiads against weirdbeards in the Middle East or fundamentalist Baptists from Virginia like Falwell? (Hitchens and Wilson 2008, 47–8)

But indignation is a form of "moral data" upon which we can reflect. We need not begin by asking for its "ultimate" ground, but by seeking its more immediate supports. Consider, for example, the recurring New Atheist denunciation of religion for the constraints it imposes on believers' minds. We can investigate whether or not religion in fact does this, and which forms are most likely to do so. But there is also an underlying ethical claim: that social institutions should not hamper the free development of human intelligence. We can certainly debate the ethical claim, and some might be inclined to nuance it, but it is not absurd, and we might reasonably feel that *challenges* to the claim need to be supported at least as firmly as the claim itself. Thus, those whose indignation is based on plausible ethical claims do not carry a unique "burden of proof," a one-sided obligation to provide "ultimate" grounds for those claims.

8. Society and Its Tasks

We have seen that, even in the absence of firm shared foundations, we have many reasons for respecting norms. We have also seen that we live subject to a cacophony of often contradictory normative demands. Many of these demands, upon reflection, cannot be taken seriously as *moral* demands, yet in everyday life they still confront us as imperious "oughts." Given all this, each citizen needs to be a moral theorist. But at the social level, what needs to be done? What are the tasks that a society must undertake if it would be reasonably just and humane?

But first, how are we to understand the idea of "society" undertaking something? Society should not be thought of anthropomorphically as a super-actor with a unified will and consciousness that can choose to do this or that. If society is to do something, *we* must do it. But this *we* can bring things about in different ways. At one extreme, the actions of "society" may represent the resultant of atomized private choices. At the other extreme, *we* as a society may act after the conscious deliberation of individuals chosen to represent society through a legitimate political process, a deliberation that is itself built upon a widespread culture of deliberation. The key here is not merely that a decision be reached by a formal political body, but that the decision be reached under conditions of authentic deliberation, which exist "only where word and deed have not parted company, where words are not empty and deeds not brutal, where words are not used to veil intentions but to disclose realities" (Arendt 1958, 200). If formal politics is greatly debased, even political decisions will reflect only the resultant of atomized pressures, pressures mediated through competitive political parties. In such situations, society's deliberation with itself, so to speak, must generally take place in a "public sphere" outside formal political structures.

But there is an intermediate space between these extremes of atomized action and fully articulated deliberation. A couple, or a small group, may talk and act with a concern for society and its good. The society in question has variable boundaries: at times we may be thinking of humanity, at times of our country, at times more narrowly, of our neighbourhood for example. When we turn to examine social dialogue in the next chapter it is this that we are considering: only a fraction of such dialogue takes place among the politically representative organs of society. And the latter *cannot* articulate the "mind" of society if not sustained *and constrained* by a civil society steeped in deliberation.

Understanding society in this way, we may now identify at least some of the tasks facing any society that would be just and humane. One ongoing task is to *sort out* the world of norms: to emphasize the vital ones, to distinguish moral claims from mere cultural expectations. Since people heed certain norms *in part* because of state coercion or social disapproval, clearly it is vital to have an ongoing reflection on just when such coercion or disapproval is justified. Thus, the normative sorting is not concerned with laws alone, and includes various social practices not codified by law. What commitments should bind us together in marriage? What sort of "business virtues" do we need today, and how can these be respected in a competitive economy? What "neighbourhood virtues" should we cultivate, what dispositions make neighbourhood life richer and more humane?

This sorting does not aim at a completely coherent, contradiction-free set of norms. Contradictions and tensions may be the only means by which we can keep sight of competing goods. Many situations require that we deploy values that are in tension with one another, as best we can: raising children to be respectful of legitimate authority, for example, yet also preparing them to be independent people in the world, and alert to abuses of authority. No good comes of suppressing one pole of such tensions in the name of consistency. Society's sorting of norms will also advance a second task, normative *development*. A just and humane society would be attentive to emerging claims against injustice, injustices not seen as such under a previous arrangement of norms.

A third task is *defence*. One aspect of this may be adapted from Feser's argument: in the face of people who *truly* reject the whole idea of moral behaviour, "Well, you know, we'd just better make sure such people don't win out" (2008, 219). That is, a society must be able to defend itself and its normative world in the face of *unjust* challenge.[20] But a more subtle form of defence is also vital: not against those who wish to be outside norms altogether, but a defence of ethical richness and complexity against reductionism. That is, we need to guard against "theories that tend to alienate us from our better moral intuitions" (Habermas 1993, 76). Given the multiple supports of our ethical life, we need to resist any belief system that isolates us from our ordinary moral intuitions, or from our "gut reactions." Our everyday ethical knowledge tells us that it is wrong to hurt others gratuitously, to kill or rob them, and so on. But an overarching belief can emerge that in one way or another deadens that moral sense. This might be a religious belief that says that those "outside," or those who have left the one true faith, are no longer "brethren" or "neighbours" towards whom we have moral obligations. It can equally well be a secular belief that we're carrying out the "task of history," or that our "scientific" ethics dispense us from the need to heed our antiquated conscience or moral intuitions, or even that our *obligation* to "find ourselves," to "self-actualize," dispenses us from ordinary human commitments. Rather than argue about which of these overarching beliefs has historically done the most damage to our moral intuitions, we need to be aware of the danger and counter it today, in whatever guise it presents itself.

Finally, a society must be able to *transmit* this moral world from generation to generation, and to sustain it as a lived world, partly by linking it to various motivations discussed above. Again, we must avoid misplaced concreteness concerning both "society" and the "moral world": what is transmitted from generation to generation will vary throughout any given society, because the transmission is not performed by society as a whole, though we should also expect considerable overlap in the "moral worlds" of members of society.

So a just and humane society must sort, develop, defend, and transmit its moral world. Such a society will fulfil these responsibilities, *in part*, through dialogue. Only in part, because the case for certain moral norms, and for ways of life, is best made simply by living them. Indeed, in the absence of this, norms will remain abstract and lifeless, lacking any power to attract allegiance. Still, dialogue is a vital means through which a society can fulfil its moral tasks. The next chapter will consider such ethical dialogue.

9. Summary of Claims

As we have ranged widely in this chapter, it will be helpful to summarize its central claims.

(1) We have no shared moral foundations. This is a falsifiable claim, yet it cannot be falsified by an isolated theoretical argument, but only by demonstrating in practice that a specific set of principles can function as a shared foundation.

(2) There is a great danger, not in the search for shared foundations, but in the belief that, absent those foundations, morality is purely subjective and arbitrary.

(3) We have a variety of reasons for respecting norms, and these reasons can function without foundations.

(4) In the face of radical challenge to the standard supports for normative behaviour, foundations offer little help.

(5) We are subject to a tangle of norms. Imperatives, many of which bear no relation to any recognizable and defensible moral code, are aimed at us from a variety of sources.

(6) This welter of demands confronts us with the task of identifying the *oughts* that we really should accept as imperative.

(7) A person's normative foundation may help advance this task, but that foundation will be more complex than one might spontaneously believe. This individual moral foundation, whatever its source, must remain "permeable" to insights arising from concrete situations.

(8) A non-foundationalist understanding of how we address the welter of normative demands can be gleaned from the metaphor of a "fabric" of beliefs. Such a fabric has no starting-point, and it is not fully "transparent," even to the person holding it. At the social level, beliefs can have unforeseen implications that only emerge over time.

(9) That our beliefs form a fabric suggests that there need be no conversation-stoppers, that there is always something to talk about, if we are willing to go on talking.

(10) The analysis points to a variety of normative tasks that must be undertaken by a just and humane society: it must sort, develop, defend, and transmit its moral world.

chapter eight

Ethical Dialogue

We ended the previous chapter noting that a just society must work on its normative fabric, in part through dialogue. Though norms can be sustained and transformed simply by living them, a just and humane society requires ongoing ethical dialogue. This chapter will begin by reflecting on the nature of that dialogue, its goals, and its associated skills and virtues. We will then consider the problem of "public reason": is it acceptable to advance "faith-based" arguments in all contexts? I will argue that it is not, and undertake the possibly hopeless task of persuading the believer who yearns for a "godly nation" to accept the sorts of restraints on discourse advocated by John Rawls. Finally, I will critique the position of those who reject the democratic premises of the arguments for broad ethical dialogue, and who encourage believers to seek some form of withdrawal from society.

1. Ethical Dialogue and Its Objectives

We can clarify the nature of the sort of ethical dialogue we need by contrasting it with the form envisioned in Habermas's discourse ethics. Ethical dialogue, first, need not involve "all possibly affected persons" (Habermas 1996, 107). It can take place between two people, or within groups of varying size, on the web, through the media, in legislatures, and so on. It can be carried on very publicly by newspaper columnists, or privately by family members around the dinner table. It is ongoing; it takes place anywhere people are willing to reflect with others on what is right and wrong, to give reasons for their beliefs, and to listen respectfully to the reasons of others.

The *scope* of the dialogue is flexible. It can touch on norms by which all might live, but also on norms that are specific to particular contexts: medical ethics, the ethics of the public servant, the norms of a particular family, and so on. Indeed, dialogue on such questions may enjoy much more concreteness for participants than dialogue on what we might term "citizen ethics." By extension, ethical dialogue can occur within particular religious groups concerning the specific norms of the group.

But conditions apply. Dialogue must involve a real difference between the parties: mutual reinforcement by the like-minded is not ethical dialogue. Discussion among the like-minded can in fact make authentic dialogue with those who think differently *more* difficult, by polarizing and entrenching attitudes (Myers 1975). And even the most intimate dialogue must have a concern for the good of the society outside the immediate encounter.

In contrast to Habermas's view that participants in rational discourse proceed with an eye to reaching agreement (1984, 42), we must recognize that people often dialogue without any clear sense of whether agreement is possible, or is even the objective. Paradoxically, dialogue will often be aided by *not* aiming at agreement. We may experience moral dialogue as frustrating and apparently fruitless precisely when we set out to *win*, to persuade another person of the rightness of our position. When our interlocutor does the same, defensiveness sets in on both sides. We may better be able to discuss openly and honestly if we accept that "victory," or even agreement, need not be the outcome of serious dialogue.

On the other hand, we do need a sincere interest in understanding each other and a commitment to the effort required for that: the discussion should be more than simply entertainment. We may thus succeed in exploring the reasons for our differences, identifying some of the beliefs that we share, and coming to understand the reasonableness of each other's position. In a world where disagreements on moral issues can turn very ugly, mutual understanding is no small achievement, even if complete agreement eludes us.[1] And we need something else, beyond a commitment to understanding: an openness to change. Without that, ethical dialogue is reduced to a toothless process of "values clarification" that tacitly accepts whatever values anyone happens to hold. Understanding and change are linked. We noted in the previous chapter that our own fabric of beliefs is not completely transparent to us. Ethical dialogue may well result in a better understanding, not just of another's beliefs, but of our own. And as we come to identify the supports and assumptions that lie behind a particular judgment, our position may evolve, even if differences with our dialogue partners remain.

Ethical dialogue starts from where we are. Philosopher of science Otto Neurath's striking image of how we advance in knowledge is relevant here: "We are like sailors who on the open sea must reconstruct their ship but are never able to start afresh from the bottom. Where a beam is taken away a new one must at once be put there, and for this the rest of the ship is used as support. In this way, by using the old beams and driftwood, the ship can be shaped entirely anew, but only by gradual reconstruction" (1973, 199). Knowledge in general, and science in particular, does not start from nowhere. A theory can only be tested by treating other theories as "unproblematic background knowledge" (Lakatos 1970, 106). Without this acceptance of some theories as solid, the scientist would have no justification for calling other theories into question. But that acceptance itself is open to revision. The "beams" upon which we rely when replacing one beam may themselves have to be replaced at another moment.

Neurath's image applies to ethical dialogue. It does not start from scratch: it takes our existing fabric of beliefs as a starting point. Our whole fabric: ethical dialogue is not just about ethical propositions. It will draw on both factual and normative beliefs, since they are intertwined in our fabrics. Participants in dialogue, of course, never hold identical fabrics of belief: that's one of the things they talk about, on an "as needed" basis. But just as a scientist could not proceed without granting a provisional assent to some theories, participants in an ethical dialogue rely on matters on which they agree in order to debate norms on which they don't, and *they cannot proceed otherwise*. Thus, however heated moral arguments may become, our situation is not like that of someone trying to communicate with aliens from another planet. We are instead like speakers of a shared language, who differ on the meaning and use of particular terms.

To summarize: ethical dialogue can take place between two people, or in a group, or in a much broader setting. It need not aim at agreement, though it must seek to advance understanding. It does not seek systematically to *ground* or *test* existing ethical norms in general, though it may well challenge established ethics here and there. Thus, ethical dialogue is in many ways a rather modest affair.

Yet the dialogue can also be sweeping. There is no reason why it cannot address questions concerning the "greatest thing, a good life and a bad one" (*Republic* 578c), given that every conception of a good life is part of a fabric of beliefs, and hence open to discussion. Some may hold that such questions cannot conclusively be resolved. But as we have seen, even a dialogue that doesn't lead to shared conclusions can be of great value. Yet for very practical reasons discussion of what constitutes a good life does not enjoy priority over ongoing reflection concerning the rules with which we will live together: we're always already immersed in society, and the various dialogues we undertake are both motivated and constrained by that fact.

2. The Skills and Virtues of Dialogue

Ethical dialogue clearly requires virtues and skills. As Jeffrey Stout argues: "There are people who lack civility, or the ability to listen with an open mind, or the will to pursue justice where it leads, or the temperance to avoid taking and causing offense needlessly, or the practical wisdom to discern the subtleties of a discursive situation. There are also people who lack the courage to speak candidly, or the tact to avoid sanctimonious cant, or the poise to respond to unexpected arguments, or the humility to ask forgiveness from those who have been wronged. Such people are unlikely to express their reasons appropriately, whatever those reasons may be" (2004, 85).

Now virtues and skills can only develop through their practice. This is one reason why ethical dialogue can seem alien and threatening to some people. Matters are not helped when issues such as the justice of modern war or the legitimacy of abortion are presented as typical examples of normative controversy (MacIntyre 1984, 6). To tackle such issues within a life relatively unshaped by ethical dialogue is akin to a novice pianist jumping from "Chopsticks" to a Rachmaninoff prelude. Nor are matters helped if we have been exposed mostly to "discussions that mimic war" (Foucault 1994, 3: 718). Nevertheless, underlying the virtues and skills of dialogue is something immediately accessible to anyone: the willingness to reject the dogmatic certainty that I am right in all respects, that those who disagree are stupid or malevolent, that I have nothing to learn from them.

Yet there is a danger that dialogue can simply reproduce dogmatism at another level: a group of people reaches an agreement, and is convinced that *now* they have laid hands on something certain. Just as the scientist should always recognize the distinction between *true* and whatever the current consensus of scientists may be, so should participants in ethical dialogue recognize that, despite their best efforts, they may go astray. Norms are not made correct simply because dialogue has endorsed them.

There is thus a tension built into serious dialogue. Dialogue *is* dialogue, and as such is dependent on the resources that the parties bring to it. At the most, it might show, "not that some position is correct absolutely, but rather that some position is superior to some other" (Taylor 1989, 72). But if a true claim is one "able to withstand any objection whatsoever" (MacIntyre 1988, 71), and not merely the objections that arise within any particular dialogue, then dialogue would seem unsuited to arriving at truth.[2] Here again an analogy with science may be helpful. A community of scientists may be strongly committed to truth, yet particular scientific theories are embraced in "dialogic" fashion, in that their fate depends upon their relation to other existing theories. While, in the abstract, their truth status depends upon their being able to survive "any objection whatsoever," in practice they must address problems and objections that arise from their immediate scientific context.[3]

If the true claim is one that can withstand any objection whatever, then the partition between true and untrue can only decisively be made from the viewpoint of eternity. In the meantime, we must act. In science, as we have seen, we proceed by taking as true theories that may yet prove otherwise. The essential thing is that *science continues*. Similarly, the essential thing is that ethical dialogue itself continue. So the spirit of reasonableness must be sustained: its purpose is not to lead us to dialogue on a "one-off" basis. At its best, ethical dialogue, like serious science, is "Janus-faced" (Habermas 1993, 146): it takes place in specific contexts with specific parties, yet those parties know that any specific dialogue is part of an ongoing dialogue, a broader stream that can embrace any context and anyone willing to take part.

3. With What Reasons Can We Reason Together?

I have given a very general sketch of a form of ongoing ethical dialogue, one that seeks to address the ethical tasks facing any society, and I have argued that a just and humane society depends upon the development of the skills and virtues of dialogue. As Stout argues, "One thing a democratic people had better have in common is a form of ethical discourse, a way of exchanging reasons about ethical and political topics" (2004, 6).

Some Christian writers reject all this. Some, first, view dialogue as pointless: "Where ordinary commonsense judgments about what is real and what is right are concerned, there is almost no common ground left between religious believers and secularists," claims Feser (2008, 227). Were this true, dialogue could hardly get off the ground. But this claim, I think, can be disposed of within the practice of dialogue itself, if one consciously seeks out the ground one shares with one's opponents. Another concern, however, merits careful consideration: in some quarters, talk of respectful dialogue and of democratic interchange is viewed as liberal code for the suppression of religious argument. Stanley Hauerwas is an influential exponent of this view: Christians, he complains, "police their convictions":

> They cannot appear in public using explicit Christian language since that would offend other actors in our alleged pluralist polity. But if this is genuinely a pluralist society, why should Christians not be able to express their most cherished convictions in public? If we are in an age of identity-politics, why does the identity of Christians need to be suppressed? Pluralism turns out to be a code word used by mainstream Christians to the effect that everyone gets to participate in the democratic exchange on his or her own terms, except for Christians themselves. (1994, 93)[4]

This section will consider the sorts of reasons with which we may reason together in various contexts. It will agree with the view that respectful dialogue requires self-restraint in one's reason-giving, and make a case for this self-restraint, while arguing that it applies only in specific situations.

Let us first consider a formulation that seems to justify Hauerwas's concern. As noted in the previous chapter, Richard Rorty once held that religion is a "conversation-stopper." Rorty thus hoped to "privatize" religion, "making it seem bad taste to bring religion into discussions of public policy" (1999, 171). This blanket prohibition on religious reason-giving relies on the incorrect assumption that conversation must end when religious reasons are advanced. And it would rule out precisely the form of honest ongoing dialogue that we need.

John Rawls's "idea of public reason" (IPR) is less easily dismissed.[5] The IPR holds that, *within a specific sphere*, and when dealing with "matters of constitutional essentials and basic justice," we should make use of justifications that depend only on "presently accepted general beliefs and forms of reasoning found in common sense, and the methods and conclusions of science, when

these are not controversial." That is, "we are not to appeal to comprehensive religious and philosophical doctrines,"[6] nor to disput-
ed approaches such as "elaborate economic theories of general
equilibrium." We are to rely instead, "as far as possible ... on
the plain truths now widely accepted, or available, to citizens in
general" (1996, 224–5).

Rawls identifies the sphere in which the IPR is to apply as the
"public political forum" (1997, 767). "Public" here does not denote
"in public," open to general observation. Rather, Rawls's meaning
parallels the usage in "public sector" or "public servant": "public"
is closely related to state institutions. So the IPR applies above all
to judges, government officials, and lawmakers, and to "candidates for public office and their campaign managers" (1997, 767).
But it also applies to ordinary citizens when they "engage in political advocacy in the public forum" (1996, 215). And in elections,
citizens are expected to "repudiate government officials and candidates for public office who violate public reason" (1997, 769). This
is because the only way to uphold the IPR among politicians is to
take away the incentive to violate it.

For Rawls, the constraints of public reason reflect our "duty of
civility to one another and to other citizens" (1997, 769). Public reason is the reason of citizens who "exercise final political and coercive power over one another" (1996, 214). It is *unreasonable*, in
deciding how that power is to be wielded on fundamental matters,
for some citizens "simply to insist on their own beliefs when they
have the political power to do so" (61).

The constraints entailed by Rawls's IPR have been exaggerated
by some commentators. James Stoner claims that "when philosophers, following John Rawls, speak of 'public reason' as the test of
what arguments and what positions are valid in public, they mean
to subject public discourse to the censorship of the secular professoriate. They know, I think, that they will never actually suppress
the voice of faith in everyday politics, but they mean to exclude it
from the higher reaches of the law, from journalism and the media,
from professional and corporate networks, and the like" (2006).
Stoner has things backwards. Rawls's conception *is* to apply to "everyday politics," to contests for public office, legislative discussions,

where the use of binding state power is at issue. Even there, there is no question of "censorship" by a "professoriate": the IPR is a moral restraint (Rawls 1997, 769) that can only be sustained by citizens in general who endorse its underlying value of civility. And it *cannot* apply to broad spheres of public debate.

Why not? Rawls's IPR holds that in the public political forum we are to appeal to generally acceptable reasons. But *how do we know* just which reasons are and are not generally acceptable? For that, we need a free interchange of reasons in our ongoing discussions outside the public political forum. As I have stressed, the fabric of our beliefs is not transparent to us, hence we may not understand the assumptions that underpin some of our reasons. Some of these reasons may seem entirely commonsensical and uncontroversial to us, but turn out to be highly problematic for others who do not share our underlying assumptions.

This problem is missed if we think that Rawls's IPR seeks to constrain only religious reasons, because we generally feel we can easily recognize religious arguments. But Rawls's IPR is to apply to *all* comprehensive doctrines. For Rawls, utilitarianism is the most influential non-religious comprehensive doctrine. Applying the IPR to it has surprising implications. Cost-benefit analysis (CBA), one of the most influential policy tools of our day, is the crooked offspring of utilitarianism (MacIntyre 1992). CBA explicitly assesses the value of anything on the basis of the market decisions of people *as they are now*, with whatever preferences they happen to have, reflecting whatever influences they happen to have undergone.[7]

The tricks by which the cost-benefit analyst moves from individual preferences to firm monetary values are often quite clever, leading to "objective" calculations of the value of clean air, health, and life itself. But can preferences often shaped by ubiquitous advertising, the desire to "get ahead," and a commitment to "conspicuous consumption" really provide a defensible standard of valuation? A common reply is: maybe not, but they're all we've got. CBA thus assumes the subjectivity of all values, their lack of relation to anything that might transcend individuals *as they are now*. There is thus a world view hidden within the practice, and a vision of the human good: a comprehensive doctrine, in short.

Metaphysics, for Rawls, "presents an account of what there is" and, by implication, of what there *isn't* (1995, 137). What there *isn't*, for CBA, is a standard of normative judgment independent of current preferences. This claim, which seems self-evident to many today, is metaphysical.

But in the absence of searching dialogue, in which all sorts of reasons may be put on the table, there is no reason for anyone steeped in this world view to understand its problematic nature. Paradoxically, then, to respect Rawlsian constraints in the formal political sphere, we need to be quite *unconstrained* in ongoing ethical dialogues elsewhere in our culture, so that those holding a wide range of comprehensive doctrines can find their views challenged.

So we can put aside the idea that we must not argue on the basis of religious beliefs outside our homes and places of worship, and focus on the specific issue: what role may such reasons play in formal discussions of government laws and policies? Let us consider a hypothetical possibility. Sam Harris's *The Moral Landscape* laments the fact that many US states permit corporal punishment in schools. "Needless to say," he adds, "the rationale for this behavior is explicitly religious" (2010, 3). Harris provides no evidence for this claim. But let us imagine a law whose preamble began "Whereas the Good Book says, 'He who spares the rod hates his son' (Prov 13:24) ..." Many citizens, whether believers or not, would consider this highly inappropriate, whatever their views of the actual content of the law. Yet the believer who yearns for a "godly nation" views this reaction as itself symptomatic of the depraved state of our society. Are there contrary arguments that might carry any weight with such believers? Are there arguments that don't rely on a prior acceptance of political pluralism?

The same question might be asked about political rhetoric that appeals to religious identities. As was seen during Perry's and Santorum's runs for the 2012 Republican presidential nomination, Christians themselves are divided on the propriety of such rhetoric. But what arguments might influence those not committed to pluralism, those untroubled by Perry's references to Obama's "war on religion" (Camia 2011) or by Santorum's claim that the president holds a "phony theology" (Fahrenthold and Sonmez 2012)?

Let us begin with religious appeals by politicians and candidates. Citizens must remember that such actors are in a "transactional relation" with us. They seek something from us, our support, and they offer us something or other in return: policies we support, a material or symbolic benefit, or perhaps just the promise of one. They may approach such transactions in an entirely cynical spirit, or not. But just as a firm totally unconcerned with breaking even will not survive, neither will a politician totally unconcerned with political support. So the *survivors* will necessarily have an interest in profit, in one context, and political support, in the other, and that interest will often lead to cynical behaviour. Thus, even the believer with no commitment to political pluralism needs to be wary of politicians who wield religious language, just as they are wary of any sales pitch.

Further, the voter who favours "god-fearing" politicians is likely to choose candidates on the basis of superficial criteria. One often reads about the "sincerity" of this or that politician, and about the "seriousness" of their religious beliefs. But how on earth can anyone think they can judge such matters of the heart? Generally, the public can judge only *professed* religious beliefs, and the very practice of supporting "god-fearing" politicians makes professed belief an unreliable guide.[8] When many voters come to assume that Christians make more trustworthy leaders than others, they create a powerful incentive for religious hypocrisy.

Further, the dualistic world view held by such voters can lead to a dangerous tendency to ignore the need to maintain *restraints* on politicians, if the voters think a particular leader is sufficiently "godly" to be worthy of their unreserved trust. Thus, even leaving aside considerations of political pluralism, the "values voter" who gravitates towards the supposedly pious politician may be behaving *immorally*. All citizens have a moral responsibility not to be scammed by politicians, because a political transaction is very different from a market one. If I buy a "lemon" of a car, I pay the price for the error. But citizens who "buy" bad political decisions may not pay the price, which can fall instead on people in other countries, or on future generations left to clean up the mess created by an ill-conceived war or fiscal irresponsibility.

Apart from the transactional relation between citizens and politicians, the citizen who yearns for a "godly nation" must be clear-eyed about the actual state of modern politics, profoundly influenced as it is by interests with deep pockets. If religious language and arguments are allowed to permeate the formal political sphere, one should expect to see monstrosities such as laws to deregulate offshore drilling or subsidize strip mining prefaced by "Whereas the Bible tells us to subdue the earth ..." That is, a new Christendom would probably end up painting a Christian veneer over a predatory capitalist reality. Believers, especially those most tempted by the siren call of Christendom, have a *moral and religious duty* to take into consideration the arguments, some of which have been presented in this book, that contemporary capitalism is more likely to shape religion to its purposes than vice versa.

In his study of American democracy, Tocqueville argued that the continued vitality of religion in America was due to the separation of church and state (1986, 1: 437).[9] In contrast, religion found itself under attack throughout Europe, not as "the representative of God," but as "the friend of power" (444). Wherever religion seeks the support of "artificial laws" and "the powers that govern society," Tocqueville argued, it sacrifices its future for the sake of its present (439).[10]

The foregoing case avoids an appeal to values of tolerance or political pluralism. It is based instead on a different good, the good of religious integrity, and autonomy from "the powers of this world." On that basis, one can make a case for restraint upon religious reason-giving in the public political forum. The exercise thus points to the plausibility of what Rawls calls an "overlapping consensus," in which citizens holding a variety of metaphysical outlooks can come to support democracy and reasonable pluralism, not *in spite of* their own outlooks, but on the basis of them. But by basing itself upon particular religious goods, the argument has been deliberately one-sided, and should not lead us to neglect the symmetry of Rawls's position. That is, there's also a need to develop arguments against reliance in the public political forum upon secular comprehensive doctrines such as utilitarianism, a task that will not be pursued here.

4. Return to the Desert?

The argument for ethical dialogue is based on the premise that we live in a democracy in which we must share the privileges and burdens of citizenship with citizens with whom we may have deep disagreements. If one rejects the premise that democracy is to be cherished, then the case for serious dialogue is obviously weakened. Not everyone accepts the premise. Consider theologian Stanley Hauerwas's comment that "the most democratically elected leader of modern times was Adolf Hitler" (2001, 527). From this we can deduce two things. Hauerwas

(1) does not like democracy very much; and
(2) hasn't got a clue what he's talking about, with respect to Hitler and democracy.[11]

This is striking: foolish people often say foolish things. But Hauerwas is no fool. That a highly influential theologian who on many questions is tremendously insightful should have no understanding of just what democrats are defending when they defend democracy is puzzling and worrisome.

In a widely cited article, "The Democratic Policing of Christianity," Hauerwas declares, "In the name of democracy, the church wills its death." He goes on: "Does that mean I do not support 'democracy?' I have to confess I have not got the slightest idea, since I do not know what it means to call this society 'democratic.' Indeed, one of the troubling aspects about such a question is the assumption that how Christians answer it might matter. Such an opportunity of choice assumes that we are or should be rulers" (1994, 105). But the question implies nothing of the sort. It assumes that Christians are *citizens*, not "rulers," and as citizens they share responsibility for society and its choices.

If one rejects the ideal of pluralist democracy, and its corollary commitment to dialogue and cooperation with citizens holding a variety of metaphysical outlooks, just what is one's alternative? The previous section examined the dangers of one possible alternative, the quest for a "godly" nation. A rather different alternative involves some form of withdrawal from the broader society. This separatism can be generally symbolic and psychological, yet include real withdrawal from at least some aspects of society, public education and "mainstream" entertainment being two common aspects.

With this partly-symbolic-partly-real separation, the "secular," the "world," becomes Hegel's proverbial night where all cows are black. Thus, Beale declares that he "could not care less what is taught in the public schools. It's like worrying about what cattle are being taught in the meat-packing factory" (2008, 166). In like spirit, Hauerwas and Willimon ask: "What good is a peace movement that works for peace for the same idolatrous reasons we build bombs – namely, the anxious self-interested protection of our world as it is?" (1989, 89). Perhaps most disturbing is Hauerwas's comment that "Christians are people who believe that any compassion that is not formed by the truthful worship of the true God cannot help but be accursed" (2001, 619): if whatever elements of goodness might *appear* to exist in non-Christians are merely accursed simulacra of true virtues, the "world" outside the church is an undifferentiated cesspool.

This undifferentiated vision of the "world" leads to a stance that is *explicitly* irresponsible: "I would like Christians to recapture the posture of the peasant. The peasant does not seek to become the master, but rather she wants to know how to survive under the power of the master" (Hauerwas 1994, 105). Encouraging people to think of themselves this way clearly does not encourage responsible citizenship. Nor does the metaphor of Christians as "resident aliens" (Hauerwas and Willimon 1989).[12]

A moral difficulty with these metaphors of withdrawal is that states wield ultimate coercive powers. These are not exercised simply against the individual citizens encouraged by Hauerwas to see themselves as "peasants," but *in their name* against others. The strategy of psychic withdrawal almost always goes hand in hand with continued payment of taxes that support coercion at home and abroad.[13] And in North America today, the psychological withdrawal of Christians who disdain secular society is often accompanied by their support for candidates who are enthusiastic advocates of foreign military adventures. Since coercion is being exercised in one's name, there is a moral responsibility not to disengage from the sphere in which decisions are made.[14]

There is another face to the modern state that we do well to keep in mind. It is certainly easy to sneer: its bureaucratic impersonality gives credence to McIntyre's comment that being asked to die for the state is "like being asked to die for the telephone company" (1994, 303). But with all its deficiencies, the state is the *articulation* of the broadest community within which rights can be protected.[15] Citizenship defines the broadest community within which we have rights that we can *make good*.[16]

And it *is* a community, though not of the type desired by "communitarians." Despite the individualism of modern society, there are clear bonds of "citizen identification," the sense that one is connected to one's fellow citizens "in a web of reciprocal rights and obligations" (Ryan 2010, 21). This is why, for example, the death of American soldiers in Iraq is a political problem for the American government, while the death of Iraqis is generally not. The bond between citizens also helps explain Amartya Sen's striking finding that "no major famine has ever occurred in a functioning democracy with regular elections, opposition parties, basic freedom of speech and a relatively free media" (2009, 342): citizens care enough for each other that a democratic government knows it cannot survive such a catastrophe.[17]

As the community of citizens, and the state that articulates it, will often come to my assistance in times of need, and may exercise coercion in my name, I owe it more than passive disengagement. Christians in particular must reject Hauerwas and Willimon's claim that "in baptism our citizenship is transferred from one dominion to another, and we become, in whatever culture we find ourselves, resident aliens" (1989, 12). Whatever our metaphysical orientation, our citizenship is a source of privileges and moral responsibilities, and simple honesty demands that we acknowledge that.[18]

5. Conclusion

This chapter has sketched the sort of ethical dialogue required by a just and humane society. That dialogue may be small in scale or large, intimate or very public. However intimate it may be, it will be motivated by some concern for the broader society. It is also motivated by a desire to reach *understanding*, but not necessarily by an expectation of reaching *agreement*. It does not seek to ground all our norms: it more modestly focuses only on norms that for one reason or another are at issue between interlocutors.

There is no reason to expect ethical dialogue to be easy or "natural" for members of our society: dialogue requires virtues and skills that are only developed through practice, and such practice is generally lacking in our culture. On the other hand, one can begin to develop the virtues and skills of dialogue as soon as one accepts a proposition available to anyone: that one is not right in all respects, and that one may learn from others, including those with whom one profoundly disagrees.

Ethical dialogue in general should be open to many types of reason-giving. Religious reasons certainly needn't constitute "conversation-stoppers." At the same time, there is a case for argumentative restraint in particular contexts, along the lines suggested by Rawls's "idea of public reason." While Rawls himself argued for the idea by appealing to the reality of social pluralism and the norm of democratic civility, my case for argumentative restraint targeted the citizen uninterested in the norms of pluralist democracy. I argued in particular that a realistic view of our political system suggests that the welcoming of religious rhetoric and argument in the formal political sphere will likely put religion in the service of powerful interests.

Finally, the chapter critiqued the recourse to partly-symbolic-partly-real withdrawal from the broader society, which tempts believers uncomfortable with both pluralist democracy and broad ethical dialogue. It was argued that Christians are neither "resident aliens" nor "peasants" who seek only to "survive under the power of the master," but citizens, a status that carries both rights and obligations.

A final question: how might ethical dialogue fit into this world of ours? On this, we need to be realistic, avoiding the idealistic illusion that the forces shaping our society can easily be sidelined. We must thus recognize that ethical dialogue will remain a marginal activity in this world: people have lives to lead, a living to earn, and they are subject to ideological and cultural influences that have often convinced them that dialogue itself is pointless, or a frill.

But to borrow a metaphor: we may hope that respectful ethical dialogue can be the "leaven in the flour," a social practice whose positive effects can, over time, be greater than its modest status would suggest.

Conclusion: Is This Enough?

The warring camps of the New Atheist debate advance core ethical claims of the same form. Each side claims that it can put our shared ethical existence on a firm footing. For one camp, that footing requires that we embrace religious belief; for the other, that we abandon it. These claims are wrong. Wherever one's sympathies lie in the New Atheist debate, we must acknowledge that neither religion, nor science, nor the zeitgeist, nor knowledge of our mortality, nor "innate human solidarity," nor, I believe, anything else that might occur to the reader, can provide us with a *shared* ethical foundation.

But we are not thereby left with nihilism or moral chaos. We are left, rather, with the world as we find it: a messy place in which a cacophony of norms compete for our attention, in which various motives lead us to attend to normative demands. Each person faces the moral task of judging which *oughts* are truly worthy of respect. And each society faces the moral tasks of sorting out its tangle of norms, developing new normative claims, defending its ethical world, and communicating norms to a new generation. These tasks must be pursued, in part, through ongoing ethical dialogue.

But is all this really enough? Can our current welter of norms, pruned and ordered to some extent by ethical dialogue, protect us from a slide into chaos? Can it give us the "steel" to protect ourselves from external threats? Is our collective "ethical fibre" up to meeting whatever challenges the future may bring? I honestly do not know. A negative answer seems more plausible if humanity is facing both ecological crises of unprecedented scope and a profound realignment of global political and economic power. Let us examine various concerns.

1. Stability and Resistance

The last two chapters suggest that we should understand what we are up to in our ethical dialogues: we should make it clear that we are talking about our fabrics of belief, *not* drawing upon some pre-existing and immutable moral foundation. But that is precisely what we must *not* do, some may object. Yes, we may adapt our ethics over time, but the stability of our society requires that most people remain unaware of this fact. Otherwise, "large majorities would waver without clear moral signals," as conservative defender Michael Novak puts it (2008, 53). This is all the more true when we are under attack, the objection continues. Terry Eagleton warns that a "long, unruly, eternally inconclusive argument … is a source of value but also of vulnerability. A tight consensus is desirable in the face of external attack" (2009, 145).

Other defenders are more explicit concerning the external menace faced by citizens in the "West." "The secular faith in democracy and material wealth," warns Beale, "is too weak, too vague, too societally enervating, to provide the post-Christian West with the spiritual steel it requires for survival." While there is much to criticize in the Crusades, he suggests, there is much to learn from them as well: "The choice for Western society today is the same as it was 1,000 years ago: the cross or the crescent" (2008, 225). Novak echoes Beale on this point: how are we to confront "an extreme ideology such as political Jihadism, conceived in the white-hot passions of resentment and bloodlust," he asks. And he warns that "some of the most sensitive members of a secularist community are liable to make excuses for murderous opponents, out of a dread for a principled moral stand – that would be too 'absolutist.' Some are liable to plead for understanding, tolerance, appeasement. Since such persons have no standard of moral truth that they might appeal to, the danger is that they may drift into pre-emptive moral surrender" (2008, 265).

Various points may be made in response. First, it is important to recall the nature of ethical dialogue. It does not set out to remake a society's moral "system": we live on Neurath's boat, and our ethical dialogue at any given moment concerns particular beams of that boat. Dialogue should thus not leave us without "clear moral signals," as Novak fears. Second, we must recognize the danger of the "external attack" claim itself. A century ago, an influential thinker based his argument against free and open debate on a striking metaphor: "We are marching in a compact group along a precipitous and difficult path, firmly holding each other by the hand. We are surrounded on all sides by enemies, and we have to advance almost constantly under their fire." Not the best time, one might agree, to sit and chat. But the thinker in question was V.I. Lenin (rpt. 1968, 33), and the society in question *never* shook loose of the belief that free discussion must be put off until some future time. Much mischief can be done by the fear that external threats should lead us to rein in democracy and freedom.

External threats do exist, of course. The question is how best to address them, which brings us to a third point. Must we not acknowledge that "defense of our civilization" *includes* defence of our right to talk about and reflect upon the things that mean the most to us, and that the closing down of debate in a multitude of ways of varying subtlety represents at least as great a threat as "political Jihadism"? Rather than jettison our freedom in the face of real and imagined threats, perhaps we should defend our civilization for the characteristics of which we should be proudest.

2. Moral Sources

Charles Taylor articulates a more subtle concern, the problem of "moral sources." A moral source is "something the love of which empowers us to do and be good" (1989, 93).[1] The notion of *grace* is a theistic moral source. Taylor asks what might take the place of this conception in a non-theistic outlook (410).

He considers the question particularly important because "our age makes higher demands of solidarity and benevolence on people today than ever before. Never before have people been asked to stretch out so far, and so consistently, so systematically, so as a matter of course, to the stranger outside the gates" (2007, 695). Taylor is not committing the mistake of the New Atheists who claim that we *are* more moral today. But we are more likely today to face moral *demands* to be concerned for *all* human beings, for future generations, for the environment. "High standards need strong sources," and we may not have those: we may be "living beyond our moral means" (1989, 516–17).

Taylor's concern cannot be met by slogans about "innate human solidarity" (Hitchens), or a "sense of our mortality" (Harris). What is at issue is whether these can gain more than a merely intellectual assent that has little power to guide our actions. But how much can we know about the moral sources active in our world until we come to share with each other, in a non-polemical context, our own personal experiences of moral empowerment? Among the many costs of polarization between believers and non-believers, and of the caricatures with which they view each other, is that it discourages such a non-polemical sharing on deeply personal matters.

3. Ethics in Evil Times

The question concerning moral sources may be stated another way. We have examined the question of how this or that ethical approach can deal with someone who is radically evil. In practice, we rarely encounter such individuals. A more worrisome problem is how good is to survive in evil times. At the social, rather than the individual, level, it is not easy to identify *any* ethical approach, religious or otherwise, that has provided much of a bulwark against cruelty and barbarism in evil times. Germany, after all, was a predominantly Christian society before embracing Nazism. It was also a very *modern* society: no doubt its intelligentsia were well acquainted with the Darwinist ideas that should have, by some accounts, persuaded them that "each of us shares a common humanity" (Dawkins 2006, 271).

To hope that some doctrine or other might hold firm in evil times is to forget that any doctrine may be put to the service of hatred, or twisted to serve militarist ends. Even when a doctrine survives relatively unscathed, at an individual level, the restraints that it might impose upon behaviour must compete against practices of military indoctrination, "groupthink," and so on. This is not to say that a set of coherent ethical beliefs is useless. It can restrain many people from acts of barbarism. But it will rarely restrain everyone, and when relations between countries or ethnic groups are fraught, a single person's "throwing the first stone" may be enough to unleash a cycle of hatred.

This suggests that, whatever our metaphysical outlook, we have a responsibility to work for a world in which *any* decent moral framework has a chance to be effective, to guide our actions in daily practice. That is, we must work to avoid the extreme situations that provoke the sorts of atrocities with which we are now all too familiar. Our situation may be illuminated by a long-standing counsel concerning virtue and prudence: we must exercise our virtue when it is strong enough to meet the challenge at hand; if we do not, we will eventually face a challenge that overwhelms us (Rousseau rpt. 1972, 1: 96–7). A wise person "will avoid, as much as duty and propriety will permit, the situations for which he is not perfectly fitted," as Adam Smith put it (2009, 289). We are not "perfectly fitted" for evil times, so we must work to prevent those times from arising. If we do not, we cannot responsibly expect our ethical beliefs, whatever their nature, adequately to deliver us from evil.

So: is this enough? I do not think that our future depends on how many people profess to follow a Christian ethics, or a Buddhist ethics, or one based on "our common humanity" (Harris), or on "mutual interest and sympathy" (Hitchens). Our future depends instead on our having the wisdom to avoid developments that test our "ethical fibre" beyond its limits, the wisdom to prevent the festering and outbreak of intense group hatreds, and the wisdom to avoid widespread environmental breakdowns that would foster a "war of all against all."

I do not suppose that we can design a utopia in which the whole problem of ethics and virtue would be overcome by social engineering, a system "so perfect that no-one will need to be good" (Schumacher 1974, 18). But we are surely capable of making a world in which, as Peter Maurin once put it, it is a little easier to be good.

Notes

Introduction

1 "But this," Hitchens glumly adds, "religion is ultimately incapable of doing" (2007, 13).

2 Elsewhere, Dennett states his goal rather differently: "The lion is beautiful but dangerous; if you let the lion roam free, it would kill me; safety demands that it be put in a cage. Safety demands that religions be put in cages, too – when absolutely necessary" (1995, 515).

3 This is most explicit with Dawkins, whose *God Delusion* has the trappings of a self-help book, with its appendix listing "friendly addresses, for individuals needing support in escaping from religion."

4 Beale's *The Irrational Atheist* is published under the surprising pseudonym "Vox Day," homonym of *Vox Dei*, or "Voice of God." I refer to him in this work by his real name.

5 The New Atheists critique religion in general, and specific religions, Christianity and Islam being their targets of choice. I am not competent to assess those aspects of the New Atheist debate touching upon Islam. As I agree with Terry Eagleton that "it is better to be provincial than presumptuous" (2009, 3), the "defenders" considered in this book are generally rooted in the Christian tradition. David Berlinski, who identifies himself as a "secular Jew," is an exception, but his response to the New Atheists stays at the level of religion in general.

6 Rawls comments in his *Political Liberalism* that, before the "successful and peaceful practice of toleration in societies with liberal institutions there was no way of knowing of that possibility." It was hence quite natural to believe that intolerance was "a condition of social order and stability"

(1996, xxvii). My study of some of the more overwrought attacks on Canadian multiculturalism (Ryan 2010), and my reading of many of the screeds penned in the New Atheist debate, suggest that many people have returned to the view that social stability requires intolerance.

7 Nor has Beale been a model of restraint in his response to individual New Atheists: Dawkins is a "supercilious old fart"; Harris is "shamelessly intellectually dishonest," displaying "all the elegance of a drunken orangutan"; Onfray has a "superlative atheist talent for assholery"; and Hitchens is "snide, petty, self-righteous, and superficial" (2008, 68, 115, 98, 198, 178).

8 The recurring insinuation that the New Atheists are intellectually deficient is puzzling. It is certainly true that the New Atheists could not have written the books they did had they chosen seriously to take into account many obvious objections to the arguments they deploy. But they chose otherwise, and to attribute this choice to stupidity is to forget that rhetoric can be most effective precisely when it refuses to acknowledge complexity.

9 The driving of the money changers from the temple is the only Gospel depiction of Jesus using physical violence. Is violence really D'Souza's preferred approach to the New Atheist debate? If not, why the choice of metaphor?

10 *Schenk v. United States*, 249 U.S. 47 at 52 [1919].

11 "In the name of democracy," declares theologian Stanley Hauerwas, "the church wills its death" (1994, 104). How so? Because in a pluralist democracy, "Christians police their own convictions to insure none of those convictions might cause difficulty for making democracy successful" (105).

12 Note the modus operandi here: those who disagree with his outlook are simply "dishonest."

13 The belief structure of those who planned and executed the September 11, 2001 barbarities had *something* to do with what they did. It is unlikely, however, that a useful explanation can take their beliefs as a sufficient cause, as most of the New Atheists assume.

14 As Pascal noted: it is custom "that makes so many Christians, that makes Turks, pagans, tradespeople, soldiers" (rpt. 1972, para. 252).

15 Of course, we do no favours to the stranger when we neglect to correct, when possible, egregious errors. To do this, we need a strong understanding of our own language (or discipline), partly in order to be able to explain the error, but also to be able to discern the difference between serious and trivial errors.

16 I refer the biblical scholar in particular to Hitchens's breathless announcement of the "shocking" truth concerning the eighth chapter of the Gospel of John, and the "astonishing" news about the conclusion to the Gospel of Mark (2007, 122, 142). The scholar would do well to acknowledge that Hitchens's understanding of biblical scholarship, such as it is, is now quite widely disseminated.

1. Charges and Defence: An Overview

1 Dawkins is not talking about this or that particular faith, but about faith as such. Hostility to critical thought is not an aberration, but part of faith's very essence: "Religious faith is an especially potent silencer of rational calculation ... because it discourages questioning, *by its very nature*" (2006, 306; emphasis added).
2 Others will doubt whether the "scriptural documents of all the great world religions" provide a clear and unanimous message on *anything*.
3 And what of children baptized as infants? "Since they already have the light of faith, it would be wrong for them to entertain doubts about whether the faith is true" (Crean 2007, 149).
4 This is a popular argument among the defenders, showing up also in Ward (2007, 192, 40) and Crean (2007, 119). The argument also turns up in a different context. Summarizing a debate between Christopher Hitchens and Tariq Ramadan, Walter Owen reports the latter's argument that religion has been "instrumentalized" by bad people, and that "Islam is a religion for human beings. But we are not peaceful human beings" (2010).

2. Faith, Reason, Radical Evil

1 It is no thanks to religion, insists Harris, that "people of faith have created almost everything of value in our world." Since, throughout history, nearly everyone has been a believer, "there has been simply no one else to do the job" (2004, 108). To those who think that religion should be "given credit for, say, the Sistine Chapel or Raphael's *Annunciation*," Dawkins replies: "Even great artists have to earn a living, and they will take commissions where they are to be had" (2006, 86).
2 As Shakespeare's Richard III put it:
   I clothe my naked villainy
   With odd old ends stol'n forth of holy writ,
   And seem a saint when most I play the devil. (1.3)

3 The argument shows up in current defenders as well. Ward, for example, argues: "It is not religion that causes intolerance. It is intolerance that uses religion to give alleged 'moral' support to the real cause of intolerance – hatred of those perceived or imagined to be oppressors or threats to one's own welfare" (2007, 38).

4 Of the New Atheists considered in this book, only Dennett avoids the issue.

5 Dawkins cites historian Alan Bullock's *Hitler* in support of his claims. He is unwilling to cite, however, Bullock's considered opinion that "In Hitler's eyes Christianity was a religion fit only for slaves; he detested its ethics in particular. Its teaching, he declared, was a rebellion against the natural law of selection by struggle and the survival of the fittest" (1962, 389).

6 Onfray's book is reference-free, so it is unclear just where he thinks he found his information on Speer. The index to Speer's memoirs contains one entry under "Christianity, Hitler on." The indexed passage cites Hitler verbatim: "It's been our misfortune to have the wrong religion. Why didn't we have the religion of the Japanese, who regard sacrifice for the Fatherland as the highest good? The Mohammedan religion too would have been much more compatible to us than Christianity. Why did it have to be Christianity with its meekness and flabbiness?" (1970, 96).

7 Many, including the New Atheists, similarly took bin Laden at his word when he claimed that his motivation for committing mass murder was fundamentally religious. It is puzzling in the two cases that such repugnant murderers should be tacitly assumed to be paragons of honesty and sincerity.

8 During the campaign, Bullock notes, opposition party meetings "were broken up, their speakers assaulted and beaten." According to official figures, fifty-one people were killed during the campaign (1962, 260).

9 The bishops' declaration did mention in passing that they were not "lifting the earlier condemnation of certain religious and moral errors" (qtd. in Wolf 2010, 168). But these "errors" were no longer seen as an impediment to Catholic participation in the Nazi party.

10 At war's end, Pius XII (1945) described the years he had lived in Germany as having been dedicated to "consolidation of the status of the Catholic Church in Germany," so he may well have seen the 1933 concordat, which he negotiated as papal secretary of state, as a coming to fruition of his efforts.

11 There was an international cost as well. Martyn Housden notes that "The Concordat was the very first international treaty signed by Hitler's government and conferred a certain respectability upon it" (1997, 53).

12 Victor Klemperer's journal of the Nazi years, *I Will Bear Witness*, repeatedly shows how fear of Bolshevism led ordinary Germans to tolerate the Nazis (1998). This suggests a lesson from the Nazi era, one overlooked in the polemical references to that horror throughout the New Atheist debate: not about the dangers of religion or atheism, but about the danger of fear, a fear that itself leads to the gradual acceptance of tyranny. This is not an irrelevant lesson today.

13 Beale offers a disturbing defence of acquiescence to the Holocaust: "How can the Catholic Church be held responsible for failing to defend those who reject its authority over them?" (2008, 202). As any good attorney knows, there are lines of defence that are more damaging to one's client than simply pleading guilty. This is one of them.

14 As the young Hegelians detected religion everywhere, "The world was sanctified to an ever-increasing extent," Marx and Engels sarcastically comment. This concept stretching, it should be noted, is a game that anyone can play. Keith Ward, for example, declares that "the clue to understanding Jihadist Islam is to see that it is a form of Islamicised Marxism" (2007, 59). The "Marxism is really religion" argument is simply inverted: "Violent religion is really Marxism."

15 Thus, one of Abel's informants wrote that "the joy of fighting for Hitler's principle gave my life a new meaning. The philosophy of the movement endowed my hitherto aimless life with a meaning and a purpose" (1965, 146). Another spoke of Hitler with strikingly religious imagery: "His conviction upheld us, whenever we weakened amidst our trials; we leaned upon him in our weariness" (153).

16 For the believer, this points to the truth of religion, as "our hearts find no peace until they rest" in God, as Augustine put it (rpt. 1961, para. 1.1). But one might also hold that "evolution had played a cruel trick on the human race, and given us an unquenchable thirst for transformation to which no objective possibility corresponded" (Taylor 2007, 819).

17 Proust suggests that rather than one person loving another because of who she is, one simply "desires to take part in the most general emotions of love," a desire that happens to attach itself to one person or another (1992, 75). Love, then, is a relation of the self to itself: those we love are simply "a product of our temperament, an image" (1988b, 456). How, precisely, are we to *disprove* that claim?

18 See also Harris (2010, 37, 203).

19 This is the point of de Beauvoir's mention of the ambiguity of the verb *to be*. The racist will say "Members of group X *are* inferior, as permanently as two is less than three." The anti-racist can answer "*If* members of group X are inferior, in certain particular respects, at this particular moment, it is the result of a history of injustice, and can be reversed."

20 Tocqueville also seemed to share Kant's view of the "fair sex": in his *Ancien régime*, he expresses astonishment that even "women and peasants" were caught up in the excitement of new philosophical ideas (rpt. 1988b, 231).

21 As Virginia Woolf commented in her caricature of "Professor von X": "Possibly when the professor insisted a little too emphatically upon the inferiority of women, he was concerned not with their inferiority, but with his own superiority. That was what he was protecting rather hot-headedly and with too much emphasis, because it was a jewel to him of the rarest price" (rpt. 1989, 34).

22 Harris's refusal to acknowledge this carries him to rhetorical extremes: "When we consciously reflect on what we *should* do, an angel of beneficence and impartiality seems to spread its wings within us: we genuinely want fair and just societies" (2010, 59).

3. Clashing Caricatures

1 It is no coincidence that Dennett and others have hit on "bright" as a new label for the atheist (2003).

2 As *Yes Minister*'s Sir Humphrey put it: "Theology's a device for helping agnostics stay within the church" (Lynn and Jay 1989, 222). Exactly how the hick believers hit on such a clever trick is unclear.

3 Dawkins is confident that unbelievers were less likely than believers to riot during the infamous Montreal police strike of 1969 (2006, 229). I lived in Montreal at the time, and I don't recall anyone making this connection. Believers in the media and justice system must have hushed up the damning truth.

4 As Taylor puts it, "The pure love of truth, uncoloured by any passionately held beliefs, is a reality of some other universe, not ours" (2007, 332).

5 The 2001 ARIS study found that the ratio of Married to "Divorced or Separated" was 2.1 among atheists (19% vs. 9%), and 6.5 for the American population in general (59% vs. 9%) (Kosmin and Mayer 2001).

6 Is this unfair? After all, Dennett has written quite a bit, and perhaps this is just one slip. But his *Breaking the Spell* is marked by a powerful *will to*

certainty thanks to which speculative musings are very quickly turned into statements of "fact." Dennett notes, for example, that both humans and animals frequently adopt an "intentional stance," which "treats something as an *agent*, with beliefs and desires." This stance, Dennett points out, is vital, since it allows an animal to recognize predators as such. But the intentional stance can also go into overdrive, as when I come to believe that Windows Vista is a malignant force seeking to drive me crazy. The "hyperactive agent detection device" (HADD), then, attributes agency when it is not warranted (2006, 109–10). In the subsequent pages, Dennett presents no evidence that HADD explains the emergence of religion. But then the reader is suddenly confronted with a chapter summary declaring, "At the root of human belief in gods lies an instinct on a hair trigger: the disposition to attribute *agency* – beliefs and desires and other mental states – to anything complicated that moves" (114). Similar transformations of speculative hypotheses into clear fact occur elsewhere in his reconstruction of the history of religion (115, 123).

7 The Bible itself acknowledges that unbelief is often provoked by believers themselves (e.g., Rom 2:24, 2 Pet 2:2).

8 Conservative believers can also influence the content of whatever sex education is offered. Thus, the Texas legislature defeated a bill that would have required sex education classes to provide medically accurate information (Collins 2011). In my province (Ontario), conservative Christians have both helped scuttle a revised sex ed program (Corlett 2010) *and* been granted a little-known blanket right to remove their children from class should "any course conflict with a religious belief held by a parent" (Wynne 2008).

9 Conservative Christians also influence local education decisions. I do not know whether one can find statistical data that are "fine-grained" enough to compare varying rates of local influence to varying indicators of phenomena such as teen pregnancy.

10 Simplifying somewhat: Tawney understood the changes in Christian ethics as stemming from the emergence of modern capitalism, while Weber famously argued that changes in Christian doctrine itself helped create a cultural space within which the spirit of capitalism could "fight its way to supremacy against a whole world of hostile forces" (rpt. 2003, 56).

11 The "Deuterocanonical" books are included in the Old Testament of the Roman and Greek canons, but not in the Protestant one. The books were included in the ancient Greek version of the Old Testament, the Septuagint, but not in the Hebrew Bible.

12 Christian preaching could now foster "an amazingly good, we may even say a pharisaically good, conscience in the acquisition of money, so long as it took place legally" (Weber rpt. 2003, 176).

13 Today, this view has been internalized, even by those who suffer its effects. In his exhaustive study of life in the modern market economy, Robert Lane comments: "I know of no substantial evidence of guilt from engaging in market activities, though there is much shame from failing to be successful in the market" (1991, 587).

14 After citing Townsend's social views, Karl Popper provocatively suggested, "If this kind of 'Christianity' has disappeared to-day from the face of the better part of our globe, it is in no small degree due to the moral reformation brought about by Marx" (1963, 2: 200).

4. The Serious and the Wishy-Washy

1 Hitchens repeats similar claims throughout his book. Of the murderous leader of Uganda's "Lord's Resistance Army," he comments: "In order to be Joseph Kony one had to have real faith" (2007, 189). And of the Rwandan genocide, he asserts that "the worse the offender, the more devout he turns out to be" (192).

2 One of the curious aspects of Hitchens's work is his claim to be able to observe things that are inherently unobservable. Here he claims that it is easy "to spot" those guided by a "sincere" observance of scripture. How exactly does one *observe* sincerity? He also claims he can "see and hear the secret satisfaction of the faithful" when disasters strike (2007, 60).

3 Aristotle presented the other side of the coin: "Those who have done a service to others feel friendship and love for those they have served even if these are not of any use to them and never will be" (*Ethics*, 1167b).

4 Eric Voegelin offers a striking analysis of the underlying dynamic. *Any* religious organization, to be an organization at all, needs some shared perspective. Hence, if a movement would stand upon "the authority of a literary source," its leaders must train their followers so that they "will automatically associate scriptural passages and terms with their doctrine" (1952, 136). The "automatic" nature of this interpretation works to sustain the literalist illusion.

5 Imagine how American religious conservatives would have reacted in the wake of 9/11 had George Bush given a speech saying we must "turn the other cheek," "love our enemies," and so on.

6 This again suggests that, contrary to the New Atheist claim, we moderns are *more* literal-minded in our treatment of scripture than our predecessors.

5. New Atheist Ethics

1 The claim that "private vices [are] public benefits" was advanced by
   Mandeville (1732), not Smith. It is ironic that Hitchens should call on
   Smith here, since the latter denounced Mandeville's theory as "wholly
   pernicious" (rpt. 2009, 362).
2 Of the passage Hitchens cites, Amartya Sen comments: "In some schools
   of economics, the readers of Smith do not seem to go beyond those few
   lines" (2009, 186).
3 Harris later echoes Dawkins: "Despite our perennial bad behavior, our
   moral progress seems to me unmistakable. Our powers of empathy are
   clearly growing" (2010, 177).
4 This is another of the not-so-new claims of the New Atheists. In the late
   eighteenth century, Gibbon offered the "pleasing conclusion that every
   age of the world has increased and still increases the real wealth, the
   happiness, the knowledge, and perhaps the virtue, of the human race"
   (rpt. 1890, 2:582).
5 The particularly opportunistic will bend multiple traditions of thought to
   their own purposes. Thus, Hitler made God out to be a social Darwinist:
   "It is much more pleasing to God if a couple that is not of healthy stock
   were to show loving kindness to some poor orphan and become a father
   and mother to him, rather than give life to a sickly child that will be a
   cause of suffering and unhappiness to all" (1939, 338).
6 As Terry Eagleton puts it, Dawkins believes that "the twentieth century,
   by far the bloodiest century on record, was a beacon of moral progress
   because one heard less racist chitchat in bars, or at least in the kind of
   bars Dawkins is likely to frequent" (2009, 87).
7 Nassau Senior's most memorable contribution to the science of
   economics was his comment that the Irish famine "would not kill more
   than one million people, and that would scarcely be enough to do any
   good" (qtd. in Gallagher 1982, 85).
8 I focus on the ethical arguments presented in Harris's first book, marked
   by a verve and sharpness of focus notably lacking from *The Moral
   Landscape* (2010), in which the foundation of Harris's ethics shifts from
   happiness to "well-being" (1). Harris refuses to offer an *explicit* definition
   of well-being, declaring that we need not trouble ourselves with
   "semantic difficulties" (183). In one passing formulation near the end of
   the book, Harris identifies well-being as "the most positive states of
   being to which we can aspire" (183). On this basis, even the most devout
   seeker of eternal bliss could endorse the proposition that ethics is about
   "well-being," and simply add that the "most positive states of being to

which we can aspire" can only be realized in an afterlife. A starting-point this broad and undefined cannot ground the sort of science to which Harris aspires.

9 A footnote in Harris's *Moral Landscape* grudgingly acknowledges, yet minimizes, the inconvenient evidence: "Decades of cross-cultural research on 'subjective well-being' (SWB) by the World Values Survey (www.worldvaluessurvey.org) indicate that religion may make an important contribution to human happiness and life satisfaction at low levels of societal development, security, and freedom" (2010, 231). The evidence is in fact much stronger than Harris allows, and it is not limited to "low levels" of development.

10 On the question of happiness and belief, Dawkins resembles a lawyer keeping his doubts about his client's case to himself. The first "consciousness-raising message" with which he begins his book is that "You can be an atheist who is happy, balanced, moral, and intellectually fulfilled" (2006, 1). It is striking that he *has to make* a declaration like this. Were believers as miserable and atheists as bubbly as he makes out, would anyone really need their "consciousness raised" about this?

11 Again, I am letting this injunction stand in for all such limiting conditions. Precisely the same questions can be asked of Onfray's view that our happiness must not be mindless, or Hitchens's injunction that we must not seek happiness in a collective "whoop of exaltation" (2007, 16).

12 Taylor and Brown's sobering summary of psychological research states that depressed individuals "are more balanced in self-perceptions"; "appear to be less vulnerable to the illusion of control"; and "appear to entertain more balanced assessments of their likely future circumstances." Their understated conclusion is that "together, these findings appear inconsistent with the notion that accurate self-knowledge is the hallmark of mental health" (1988).

13 Someone probably drew to Harris's attention the contradiction between his definition of science in terms of "observation and experiment" and his desire to build a strictly scientific ethics, since his later books considerably broaden the definition of science. Science now "represents our best efforts to know what is true about our world. We need not distinguish between 'hard' and 'soft' science here, or between science and a branch of the humanities like history." So, "The core of science is not controlled experiment or mathematical modeling; it is intellectual honesty" (2006, 64; see also 2010, 29, 195). Whatever one thinks of his updated definition, note that it would render scientific any rigorous theology that prohibits "irrationality, unjustified reactions, subjectivist decisions," as theologian Hans Küng puts it (1981, 337).

14 Harris's position, though clothed in secular garb, is curiously close to that of Job's friends, who are scandalized by the notion that a just person might suffer.

15 The second condition is essential. Tocqueville suggested that citizens focused only upon their search for personal pleasure would tolerate the emergence of "an immense tutelary power" that would effectively freeze citizens in childhood (rpt. 1986, 2: 434). Such a state of affairs could hardly be stable: there would be a permanent temptation to convert "soft" despotism into something more malign. And, as Charles Taylor argues, "enlightened self-interest will never move enough people strongly enough to constitute a real threat to potential despots" (1995, 197).

16 Both Dawkins and Hitchens cite a letter of Thomas Jefferson's arguing that in the absence of religious belief, "you will find incitements to virtue in the comfort and pleasantness you feel in its exercise, and the love of others which it will procure you" (Dawkins 2006, 42; Hitchens 2005, 182-83). Clearly Harris is not the only New Atheist drawn to "the superstitious belief in a certain relationship between happiness and virtue" (Nietzsche rpt. 1968, 140).

  Both Dawkins and Hitchens omit the continuation of Jefferson's letter: "If you find reason to believe there is a god, a consciousness that you are acting under his eye, & that he approves you, will be a vast additional incitement" (rpt. 2006, 163).

17 Harris belongs to the "success by subtraction" school of thought. Its underlying assumption is captured by an old fable, in which Michelangelo was asked how he had managed to sculpt his David. "Easy," he replied, "I started with a block of marble and began to chip away at it. When I arrived at David, I stopped." Similarly, some believe that we can arrive at a human utopia by starting with humanity as it is, then chipping away a few things we don't like. As John Lennon's *Imagine* put it: chip away our religion, country, and property, and (presto!) we will all "live as one." Charles Taylor's *A Secular Age* repeatedly critiques such "subtraction stories" (2007, 22, 293, 572). See also Lovejoy (1964, 9).

18 As with other oracular pronouncements offered up by the New Atheist debate, this one is stale. Prince Albert, for example, declared in 1851, "Nobody who has paid any attention to the peculiar features of our present era will doubt for a moment that we are living in a period of most wonderful transition, which tends rapidly to accomplish that great end to which, indeed, all history points – the realization of the unity of mankind" (qtd. in Vickers 1965, 127).

19 During the Nazi tyranny, Victor Klemperer noted in his journal: "Curious: at the very moment modern technology annuls all frontiers

and distances (flying, radio, television, economic interdependence), the most extreme nationalism is raging" (1998, 282).

20 As we will see in a moment, our increasing interdependence has produced just such reactions in Harris himself.

21 Apart from the authoritarian spirit of all this, we should also note the implied trust in the potential for education to *work*, to transform people. This too is not new to the New Atheists. As Tocqueville said of an earlier cohort of would-be philosopher-kings, "their trust in intellectual medication ... is limitless" (rpt. 1988b, 250).

22 "Preemptive," because if Harris were solely concerned with punishing those whose beliefs had *already* led them to engage in certain barbaric actions, it would be pointless for him to declare that we are allowed to kill people because of their beliefs alone. In his *Moral Landscape*, Harris asserts that the idea of punishing people for what they have *already* done is rooted in ignorance, because "what we condemn in another person is the *intention to do harm*" (2010, 108–9). Presumably, his science-based utopia will establish a "pre-crimes unit."

23 Even while expressing horror at the prospect, Harris's language takes on an Orwellian tone, referring to a nuclear *first* strike as an act of "self-defense."

24 Harris does not repeat this argument in his later books. Nor does he retract it.

25 In a subsequent book, Harris ignores another warning signal. He declares: "With a few exceptions, the only public figures who have had the courage to speak honestly about the threat that Islam now poses to European society seem to be fascists" (2006, 85). Anyone who discovers that fascists are closest to his own views on an issue really should stop and cast a critical eye over his own thinking process. Harris does not.

26 Dennett thanks Dawkins for his "particularly valuable suggestions" (2006, xv). Dawkins thanks Dennett and Harris (2006, 7).

27 Harris draws on Hitchens and Dawkins (2006, 35, 73). Dennett calls on Harris and Dawkins (2006, 293, 78f). Hitchens leans heavily on the other New Atheists throughout his work.

28 Dennett praises Harris for his "brave book" (2006, 299). Dawkins, for his part, published a fawning review of Hitchens in the *Times Literary Supplement* (2007).

29 I have found only one explicit disagreement among the four Anglo-American writers, and that on a trivial point: Hitchens disagrees with Dawkins's and Dennett's use of the term "brights" to denote atheists (2007, 5).

30 On the issue of people being too polite to criticize each other's beliefs, the New Atheists have matters exactly backwards. We saw in chapter 1 that the defenders are quite willing to criticize other members of their "team." It is the New Atheists who are strangely reticent on this count.

31 Harris's *Moral Landscape* also attacks "The Illusion of Free Will" (2010, 102ff.). After attempting to free the reader of this "illusion," however, Harris declares, "This insight does not make social and political freedom any less important, however. The freedom to do what one intends, and not to do otherwise, is no less valuable than it ever was" (2010, 106). Why that is so Harris does not say.

32 Spinoza had earlier acknowledged that his denial of free will would not eliminate control and repression, but simply divorce them from moral reprobation: "He who goes mad from the bite of a dog is excusable, yet he is rightly suffocated" (rpt. 1992, 290).

33 Lewis issued a pertinent warning here: "We know that one school of psychology already regards religion as a neurosis. When this particular neurosis becomes inconvenient to government, what is to hinder government from proceeding to 'cure' it?" (1970, 293).

34 Ironically, Onfray attacks religion for its "obsession with purity," for its belief that a "contaminated" person "in turn contaminates everything he approaches or touches" (2007, 72).

35 Thus: "Just as the spraying of the grapevine in three stages may keep it from being attacked by downy mildew, just so the spraying of human beings with mixtures appropriate to the circumstances becomes indispensable. The schools are the first stage for this kind of spraying" (Vassilikos 1996, 6).

36 Onfray is in effect repeating the claim that "it is contrary to reason that error and truth should have equal rights," articulated by … Pope Leo XIII (*Libertas Praestantissimum*, 34).

6. The Defenders' Moral Foundations

1 One might argue that there are more than two dimensions, a complication that does not affect the argument developed in the following chapters: if we cannot identify a shared moral foundation of two dimensions, as I will argue, we are *a fortiori* unable to identify one of three or more.

2 On this, see Hauerwas (2001, 228), Taylor (1989, 3), and MacIntyre (1984, 119).

3 In this wider approach, one must also understand "do" quite broadly. Changing what I "do" can include such outwardly imperceptible things as changing the way I talk to myself, changing the way I develop awareness of my emotions, and so on. At times what I must "do" is simply to let something be done to me, to let go.

4 In the original article from which this passage is drawn, Novak wrote of "its effects on the less educated," rather than "its effects on the general run of humankind" (2007). The original wording suggests that the conservative Novak considers religion of particular value in keeping the unwashed plebes in line.

5 I am not advancing a consensus theory of ethical foundations. Rather, the claim is analogous to saying that we expect a true scientific theory eventually to be recognized as such by all competent scientists; this is not the same as saying that a consensus among competent scientists *constitutes* scientific truth.

6 Crean and Beale's explanations are in tension with one another, a tension related to Socrates's question "Is what is pious loved by the gods because it is pious, or is it pious because it is loved?" (*Euthyphro* 10a). Beale opts for the latter: the universe being "God's game," God gets to make whatever rules he wants, and the just is whatever is willed by God. In this case, Crean's statement that God is "law and wisdom itself" becomes an empty tautology, because God gets to define those qualities as he wishes. As Lovejoy noted: "If you assumed that a thing was *made* good merely by God's willing it, and evil, or not good, by his not willing it, you were debarred from reasoning at all about the implications of the attribute of 'goodness'" (1964, 70). On this, see also Wolterstorff's critique of Ockam (2008, 90).

7 When Swift's Gulliver tried to explain the idea of lying to one of the virtuous Houyhnhnms, "it was with much Difficulty that he comprehended what I meant, although he had otherwise a most acute Judgment. For he argued thus: That the Use of Speech was to make us understand one another, and to receive Information of Facts; now if anyone *said the Thing which was not*, these Ends were Defeated" (rpt. 1985, 195). Swift had no illusions concerning the potential of this natural-law understanding of speech to influence us.

8 Feser's twenty-two pages on natural law are entirely focused on sexual practices, save for the occasional mention of alcoholism. In a nice touch, he pauses in the middle of his extended natural-law denunciation of homosexuality, contraception, and abortion to complain against "the

tiresome cliché that natural law moralists are 'obsessed with sex'" (2008, 141).

9 A 2005 Gallup poll, for example, found that 78 per cent of American Catholics believed that their church should permit birth control (Moore 2005).

10 Haught relies on Paul Tillich's understanding of faith as a state of "being grasped" by "ultimate concern" (2008, 61). Perhaps it is a matter for psychologists and sociologists, rather than theologians, to assess whether such an understanding is likely to generate a widespread commitment to doing good. Indeed, Tillich himself might have been sceptical on this point, as he recognized the widespread need for "symbols that are immediately understandable without the mediation of intellect" (1948, 227).

11 Rawls most certainly does not limit himself to saying "we'd just better make sure such people don't win out." He devotes much thought to the conditions of stability of a well-ordered society, and he does so with some rigour. While one may reject his argument, it is an argument. Feser, on the other hand, fails even to address this problem.

7. Can We Live without Foundations?

1 "We cannot search the whole world in order to establish that something does not exist, has never existed, and will never exist" (Popper 2002, 49).

2 It is not clear how Berlinski travels from morality being the result of "what men and women decide" to "everything is permitted."

3 The introduction to Samuelson's influential *Economics* states: "'Beauty is in the eye of the beholder' is an aphorism reminding us that judgments of better or worse involve *subjective* valuations." Hence, economists need not address "questions concerning right and wrong goals" (1976, 7).

4 The tendency to toss around the "satanic" label has no natural stopping point. A media-savvy pastor from North Carolina garnered national headlines by announcing a Halloween night book burning, including such "satanic" works as the Bible itself! The good pastor declared that all versions of the Bible except his preferred King James version were "satanic perversions" (Associated Press 2009).

5 This means, as we shall see, that many of the motives identified can support norms that strike us as entirely negative.

6 The motivations identified are not meant to represent "levels" or "stages" of morality. If, in this or other accounts, some motivations seem "higher"

than others, we do well to remember that, for most of us, ethical constancy depends upon the cooperation of various motivations.

7   I repeat that we are here examining various motivations to respect norms, without consideration of the content of those norms, to which we turn below. A desire for self-esteem can lead one to commit evil. Consider Lady Macbeth's warning to her husband that if he does not go through with the plan to murder Duncan in his sleep, Macbeth will "live a coward in thine own esteem" (*Macbeth*, 1.7; see also *Richard III*, 1.4).

8   Cervantes offers a variation on the same theme, as Quixote gains satisfaction from his projected heroic exploits by imagining "times to come, when the true story of my famous deeds comes to light" (rpt. 1987, 80).

9   Hitchens dismisses this saying as a "piece of pointless pseudoprofundity" (2007, 133). His alliterative dismissal ignores a distinction that for many people is quite evident and important.

10   Recognizing the element of *love* for God challenges an aspect of the New Atheist understanding of belief. Hitchens asserts that the believer's morality depends upon "the impulse of terrifying punishment or selfish reward" (Hitchens and Wilson 2008, 32). But our relations with our spouse, our children, or our dearest friends, are not based on a narrow calculation of the costs and benefits of potential "punishments and rewards." Our relations with those most important to us are shaped by a variety of motives and sentiments, and so are many believers' relations with God. One may choose to dismiss that relation as a pure delusion, akin to Christopher Robin's relation with his imaginary friend Binker, as Dawkins puts it (2006, 348), but this does not erase its complexity. For anyone who doubts this, careful consideration of the range of attitudes towards God displayed in the Book of Psalms will provide a useful corrective.

11   In Joseph Heller's Second World War novel *Catch-22*, Yossarian has announced that he does not wish to fight any more. "Let somebody else get killed," he declares. In response, Major Major poses the Kantian question: "But suppose everybody on our side felt that way." Yossarian is not troubled: "Then I'd certainly be a damned fool to feel any other way. Wouldn't I?" His officer gives up: *"What could you possibly say to him?* Major Major wondered forlornly" (1961, 102).

12   Many novelists have written of this social preference for success over virtue. The hotel director in Proust's resort town of Balbec has nothing against guests who seek to spend as little as possible, so long as they do so "because of greed, not poverty" (1988b, 231). In a lighter vein, Stephen

Leacock depicts "Lenten services at noonday, when the businessmen sit in front of him in rows, their bald heads uncovered and their faces stamped with contrition as they think of mergers that they should have made, and real estate that they failed to buy for lack of faith" (1989, 132).

13 I say "a world," though to some extent each of us has our own world, in the sense that each of us represents a "unique intersection of influences" (Ryan 2010). Each person is exposed to a slightly different set of demands; the "weightings" among those demands varies, and so on. The "world," as Mill puts it, "to each individual, means the part of it with which he comes in contact" (1974, 77).

14 This formulation may provoke a question: those oughts that we really ought to heed … *why*? Different answers are possible: if we're to lead fully human lives; or perhaps, if we're to live the lives that we are *called* to live. In my view, those two answers are ultimately one, but others will insist that talk of a "call" only confuses matters.

The arguments that lead me to deny the existence of a shared moral foundation also lead me to doubt whether there can be a shared answer to this question. Despite this, it is clear that people with a wide variety of metaphysical outlooks agree that there is a distinction between moral demands that confront us as *legitimate* imperatives and other types of demands and social pressures that pose as imperatives.

15 The "cherry picking" charge is levelled by New Atheists (Onfray 2007, 160; Harris 2006, 18), demonstrating again their affinity with fundamentalist belief.

16 I'm not assuming that we can easily classify all propositions as one or the other, nor is it necessary to do so. Putnam offers "John would do anything for money" as an example of a statement not easily classified (1981, 139).

17 These observations do not assume a "coherence theory of truth." The discussion is not about truth, but about the supports for any statement. Even a false claim is supported by beliefs, and it is often those supports that create an opening to challenge the claim.

18 Rorty now acknowledges that his own commitment to utilitarianism is *also* a conversation-stopper, and comments that "instead of saying that religion was a conversation-stopper, I should have simply said that citizens of a democracy should try to put off invoking conversation-stoppers as long as possible" (2003, 148).

19 At the outset of the *Republic*, Socrates's interlocutors ask him, "Could you really persuade, if we don't listen?" (327). It is important not to confuse a refusal to dialogue with the *impossibility* of dialogue.

20 This implies that ongoing reflection on precisely what constitutes just
   and unjust challenges is also required.

8. Ethical Dialogue

1 In formal contexts where some decision must be reached, as in a
  legislature, matters will often be decided by vote long before consensus
  is reached. But when that vote has been preceded by honest debate, it is
  easier for those who disagree with the final decision to acknowledge
  its legitimacy.
2 The discussion here is not materially affected if one holds that normative
  questions do not admit of truth, but only of some "truth-analogous
  concept" such as "validity" (Habermas 1992, 75).
3 On this, diverse thinkers such as Popper, Lakatos, Kuhn, and indeed
  MacIntyre himself (2006, 10) agree.
4 Candidate for the 2012 Republican presidential nomination Rick
  Santorum put the complaint more graphically: "To say that people of
  faith have no role in the public square? You bet that makes you throw up.
  What kind of country do we live [in] that says only people of non-faith
  can come into the public square and make their case?" (2012).
5 I have considered Rawls's position in more detail in Ryan (2014).
6 A comprehensive doctrine "includes conceptions of what is of value in
  human life, and ideals of personal character, as well as ideals of friendship and of familial and associational relationships, and much else that is
  to inform our conduct, and in the limit to our life as a whole" (Rawls
  1996, 13). The concept is not limited to religious doctrines.
7 This view enjoys a long lineage. Alasdair MacIntyre notes that Callicles,
  as presented in Plato's *Gorgias*, views "the human individual with
  whatever desires he or she may have as providing the measure of value"
  (1988, 108).
8 In an early 1933 memorandum to Cardinal Pacelli, the future Pius XII,
  German cardinal Faulhaber listed among the points in Hitler's favour the
  fact that he would "proclaim the name of God" and invoke "Providence"
  in his speeches (qtd. in Wolf 2010, 162).
9 Tocqueville claimed that every American he talked to, both clergy
  and lay people, agreed on this. Times have changed.
10 Rawls cites Tocqueville's argument in his own case for the idea of public
   reason (1997, 796).
11 One can consult any history of the Third Reich to learn that the process
   by which the Nazi party moved from its 33% share of the popular vote in

the election of November 1932 to being the sole legal party in Germany by mid-July 1933 cannot be termed "democratic."

12 Hauerwas is a prolific writer, with many occasional pieces not governed by a desire for strict consistency. The passages cited here are not a summary of his thought, but simply present an important strand in that thought. Despite the metaphors of Christians as "peasants," and "resident aliens," Hauerwas himself often comments, with great insight and compassion, on a wide range of political issues. His "Pacifist Response" to the September 11 attacks is not the work of a "peasant" who keeps his head down, but of a brave and responsible thinker (rpt. 2004). Perhaps Hauerwas needs, then, to "theorize" his own practice, to draw from his own engagements insights concerning how believers might engage with their society.

13 Stout comments: "To my knowledge, [Hauerwas] has advocated neither the withholding of taxes that finance the military, nor participation in costly acts of civil disobedience, nor refusal of communion to soldiers and their commanders" (2004, 159).

14 Yet we must also be realistic about the limits to the influence of ordinary citizens in our current democracy. I do not deny, for example, that our politics today are afflicted by what Rawls terms the "curse of money" (1997, 772). This does not excuse us from engagement, but simply points to our responsibility to fight against that and other contemporary "curses."

15 In Eric Voegelin's terminology, articulation is the process by which communities become "capable of representing themselves for action": "In order to come into existence, a society must articulate itself by producing a representative that will act for it" (1952, 38, 41).

16 As Arendt notes, the Holocaust and other horrors have shown that the "rights of man" are "claimed only by people who were too weak to defend their 'rights of Englishmen' and to enforce their own laws" (1964, 271).

17 As Sen points out, this cannot be explained on the basis of individualistic self-interest: "The proportion of the population affected, or even threatened, by a famine tends to be very small – typically much less than ten per cent ... So if it were true that only disaffected famine victims vote against a ruling government when a famine rages or threatens, then the government could still be quite secure" (2009, 343).

18 One might counter this whole analysis with various New Testament verses (e.g., Phil 3:20; 1 Pet 2:11; Heb 11:13). But as argued throughout this book, a few biblical verses should not end a discussion. So we might

ask: exactly how are we to apply advice given in the first-century Roman empire to today's world?

Conclusion: Is This Enough?

1 A moral foundation was defined in two dimensions: content and motivation. Taylor's point is that the *desire* to do good and the *capacity* to do so are not the same, a truth well known to anyone who has battled an addiction.

Works Cited

Note: URLs for online news articles are transient, sometimes expiring within a few days of publication, or sending the reader to a subscription service which requires payment. For newspapers, then, I simply cite the article in the traditional way. Generally, the reader who wishes to track down such a citation can follow a number of paths: increasingly, local and university libraries offer access to news databases such as LexisNexis or Factiva. Where facsimile reproductions of books have been consulted, the reference is to the originating print edition.

Abel, Theodore. 1965. *The Nazi movement: Why Hitler came to power.* New York: Atherton Press.

Achebe, Chinua. 1959. *Things fall apart.* New York: Fawcett Crest.

Aikman, David. 2008. *The delusion of disbelief.* Carol Stream, IL: Tyndale House.

Allen, Mike. 2005. GOP congressman calls Democrats anti-Christian. *Washington Post*, 21 June.

Ambrose. 1896. "On the mysteries." In *A select library of the Nicene and post-Nicene fathers of the Christian church*, 2nd ser., vol. 10, ed. Philip Schaff and Henry Wace. Buffalo: Christian Literature Company.

Aquinas, Thomas. 1947. *Summa theologica.* New York: Benziger Brothers.

Aquinas, Thomas. 1952–4. *Truth.* Chicago: H. Regnery Co.

Arendt, Hannah. 1958. *The human condition.* Chicago: University of Chicago Press.

Arendt, Hannah. 1964. *Eichmann in Jerusalem: A report on the banality of evil.* Rev. ed. Harmondsworth: Penguin.

Arendt, Hannah. 1978. *The life of the mind: Thinking.* San Diego: Harcourt Brace.

Aristotle. 1941. *The basic works of Aristotle*. Ed. Richard McKeon. New York: Random House.

Aristotle. 1962. *The politics of Aristotle*. Trans. Ernest Barker. New York: Galaxy.

Associated Press. 2009. "NC pastor: King James is the only Bible; plans to burn Bibles and Christian books on Halloween." 15 October.

Augustine. 1866. "De Genesi ad litteram." In *Oeuvres complètes de saint Augustin*, vol. 4, ed. M. Raulx. Nancy: Thomas et Pierron.

Augustine. 1887. "Reply to Faustus the Manichean." In *A select library of the Nicene and post-Nicene Fathers of the Christian church*, vol. 4, ed. Philip Schaff. Buffalo: Christian Literature Company.

Augustine. 1888a. "On the Gospel of St. John." In *A select library of the Nicene and post-Nicene Fathers of the Christian church*, vol. 7, ed. Philip Schaff. New York: Christian Literature Company.

Augustine. 1888b. "On the Psalms." In *A select library of the Nicene and post-Nicene Fathers of the Christian church*, vol. 8, ed. Philip Schaff. New York: Christian Literature Company.

Augustine. 1961. *Confessions*. Trans. R.S. Pine-Coffin. London: Penguin.

Augustine. 1991. *On Genesis against the Manichees*. Trans. Roland Teske. Washington: Catholic University of America Press.

Ayer, A.J. 1946. *Language, truth and logic*. London: Victor Gollancz.

Bainton, Roland. 1960. *Christian attitudes toward war and peace*. Nashville: Abingdon.

Barber, Benjamin. 1992. "Jihad vs McWorld." *The Atlantic Monthly*, March.

Bates, Stephen. 2000. "Anger at India textbook bias." *Guardian Weekly*, 3 February.

Beale, Theodore [Vox Day pseud.]. 2008. *The irrational atheist: Dissecting the unholy trinity of Dawkins, Harris, and Hitchens*. Dallas: BenBella Books.

Becker, Gary S. 1981. "Altruism in the family and selfishness in the market place." *Economica*, new ser., 48 (189): 1–15.

Bellah, Robert, et al. 2008. *Habits of the heart: Individualism and commitment in American life*. Updated ed. Berkeley: University of California Press.

Berlinski, David. 2008. *The Devil's delusion: Atheism and its scientific pretensions*. New York: Crown Forum.

Berne, Linda, and Barbara Huberman. 1999. "European approaches to adolescent sexual behavior and responsibility." Washington: Advocates for Youth. <www.advocatesforyouth.org/storage/advfy/documents/european.pdf>.

Bernstein, Richard J. 1989. "Pragmatism, pluralism and the healing of wounds." *Proceedings and Addresses of the American Philosophical Association* 63 (3): 5–18.

Bethge, Eberhard. 1970. *Dietrich Bonhoeffer*. Trans. Eric Mosbacher, et al. New York: Harper and Row.

Brown, Raymond. 1968. "Hermeneutics." In *The Jerome Biblical commentary*, ed. Raymond Brown, Joseph Fitzmyer, and Roland Murphy. Englewood Cliffs, NJ: Prentice-Hall.

Bullock, Alan. 1962. *Hitler: A study in tyranny*. Harmondsworth: Penguin.

Camia, Catalina. 2011. "Perry slams Obama's 'war on religion' in new ad." *USA Today*, 7 December.

Camus, Albert. 1956. *La chute*. Paris: Gallimard.

Cervantes, Miguel de. 1987. *El ingenioso hidalgo don Quijote de la Mancha*. Madrid: Editorial Castalia.

Collins, Gail. 2011. "Mrs. Bush, abstinence and Texas." *New York Times*, 16 February.

Comité Permanente del Episcopado. 1975. Evangelio y Paz. *Mensaje* (Santiago), September.

Comte, Auguste. 1890. *Catéchisme positiviste*. 3rd ed. Paris: Larousse.

Copan, Paul. 2008. "God, naturalism, and the foundations of morality." In *The future of atheism: Alister McGrath and Daniel Dennett in dialogue*, ed. Robert B. Stewart. Minneapolis: Fortress Press.

Corlett, John. 2010. "Ontario's children lose out in sex-ed furor." *Toronto Star*, 27 April.

Cornwell, Rupert. 2006. "Jury hears the final moments of Flight 93." *The Independent*, 13 April.

Cortesi, Arnaldo. 1933. "Vatican and Reich initial Concordat: Von Papen says it renders impossible a conflict." *New York Times*, 9 July.

Crean, Thomas. 2007. *God is no delusion: A refutation of Richard Dawkins*. San Francisco: Ignatius Press.

Dawkins, Richard. 1997. "Is science a religion?" *Humanist* 57: 26–9.

Dawkins, Richard. 2006. *The God delusion*. Boston: Houghton Mifflin.

Dawkins, Richard. 2007. "Bible Belter, review of *God is not great*, by Christopher Hitchens." *Times Literary Supplement*, 5 September.

Dean, Cornelia. 2005. "A new screen test for Imax: It's the Bible vs. the volcano." *New York Times*, 19 March.

de Beauvoir, Simone. 1961. *The second sex*. Trans. H.M. Parshley. New York: Bantam.

de las Casas, Bartolomé. 1813. *Brevísima relación de la destruición de las Indias*. Bogota: J.M. Ríos.

Dennett, Daniel. 1995. *Darwin's dangerous idea*. New York: Penguin.

Dennett, Daniel. 2003. "The bright stuff." *New York Times*, 12 July.

Dennett, Daniel. 2006. *Breaking the spell: Religion as a natural phenomenon*. New York: Penguin.

Dennett, Daniel. 2007. "The monsters and critics interview." <http://www.cosmoetica.com/DSI2.htm>.

Dennett, Daniel, and Alister McGrath. 2008. "The future of atheism: A dialogue." In *The future of atheism: Alister McGrath and Daniel Dennett in dialogue*, ed. Robert B. Stewart. Minneapolis: Fortress Press.

D'Souza, Dinesh. 2007. *What's so great about Christianity?* Washington, DC: Regnery.

Eagleton, Terry. 2009. *Reason, faith, and revolution: Reflections on the God debate.* New Haven: Yale University Press.

Fahrenthold, David A., and Felicia Sonmez. 2012. "In weaving faith into campaign, Santorum resorts to chiding opponents." *Washington Post*, 19 February.

Faustus of Riez. 1975. "Sermons on the Epiphany." In *A short breviary*, ed. Monks of Saint John's Abbey. 4th ed. Collegeville, MN: Saint John's Abbey Press.

Fearon, James, and David Laitin. 2000. "Violence and the social construction of ethnic identity." *International Organization* 54 (4): 845–77.

Feser, Edward. 2008. *The last superstition*. South Bend, IN: St Augustine's Press.

Feyerabend, Paul. 1993. *Against method*. 3rd ed. London: Verso.

Fish, Stanley. 1994. *There's no such thing as free speech: And it's a good thing, too.* New York: Oxford.

Foucault, Michel. 1975. *Surveiller et punir*. Paris: Gallimard.

Foucault, Michel. 1994. *Dits et écrits: 1954–1988*. Paris: Gallimard.

Friedman, Milton. 1953. *Essays in positive economics*. Chicago: University of Chicago Press.

Friedman, Milton. 1970. "The social responsibility of business is to increase its profits." *New York Times Magazine*, 13 September.

Frye, Northrop. 1991. *The double vision*. Toronto: University of Toronto Press.

Gadamer, Hans-Georg. 1989. *Truth and method*. 2nd ed. New York: Continuum.

Gallagher, Thomas. 1982. *Paddy's lament*. New York: Harcourt Brace Jovanovich.

Gerard, James. 1933. "Hitler as he explains himself." *New York Times*, 15 October.

Gibbon, Edward. 1890. *The decline and fall of the Roman Empire*. London: W.W. Gibbings.

Gilson, Étienne. 1937. *The unity of philosophical experience*. New York: Charles Scribner's Sons.

Habermas, Jürgen. 1984. *The theory of communicative action I: Reason and the rationalization of society*. Trans. Thomas McCarthy. Boston: Beacon Press.

Habermas, Jürgen. 1992. *Postmetaphysical thinking*. Cambridge, MA: MIT Press.

Habermas, Jürgen. 1993. *Justification and application*. Trans. Ciaran Cronin. Cambridge, MA: MIT Press.

Habermas, Jürgen. 1996. *Between facts and norms*. Trans. William Rehg. Cambridge, MA: MIT Press.

Harris, Sam. 2004. *The end of faith: Religion, terror, and the future of reason*. New York: W.W. Norton & Company.

Harris, Sam. 2006. *Letter to a Christian nation*. New York: Alfred A. Knopf.

Harris, Sam. 2007. "Sam Harris strikes back." <http://www.truthdig.com/report/item/20070529_sam_harris_fights_back>.

Harris, Sam. 2010. *The moral landscape*. New York: Free Press.

Hart, David Bentley. 2009. *Atheist delusions: The Christian revolution and its fashionable enemies*. New Haven: Yale University Press.

Hauerwas, Stanley. 1994. *Dispatches from the front*. Durham: Duke University Press.

Hauerwas, Stanley. 2001. *The Hauerwas reader*. Ed. John Berkman and Michael Cartwright. Durham: Duke University Press.

Hauerwas, Stanley. 2004. *Performing the faith*. Grand Rapids, MI: Brazos.

Hauerwas, Stanley, and William Willimon. 1989. *Resident aliens: Life in the Christian colony*. Nashville: Abingdon Press.

Haught, John F. 2008. *God and the new atheism: A critical response to Dawkins, Harris, and Hitchens*. Louisville: Westminster John Knox Press.

Hebblethwaite, Peter. 1982. "The Pope and Fatima." *New Blackfriars* 63 (748): 422–9.

Hedges, Chris. 2007. "I don't believe in atheists (Debate with Sam Harris)." <http://www.truthdig.com/report/item/20070523_chris_hedges_i_dont_believe_in_atheists/>.

Hedges, Chris. 2008. *I don't believe in atheists*. New York: Free Press.

Heller, Joseph. 1961. *Catch-22*. New York: Simon and Schuster.

Helliwell, John. 2002. "How's life? Combining individual and national variables to explain subjective well-being." *National Bureau of Economic Research Working Paper*, no. w9065 (July).

Hinojosa y Naveros, E. 1908. "Bull of the Crusade." In *The Catholic Encyclopedia*. New York: Robert Appleton Company. <http://www.newadvent.org/cathen/04543b.htm>.

Hitchens, Christopher. 2005. *Thomas Jefferson: Author of America*. New York: Atlas Books.

Hitchens, Christopher. 2007. *God is not great: How religion poisons everything*. New York: Twelve Books.

Hitchens, Christopher, and Douglas Wilson. 2008. *Is Christianity good for the world?* Moscow, ID: Canon Press.

Hitler, Adolf. 1939. *Mein Kampf.* Trans. James Murphy. London: Hurst and Blackett.

Housden, Martyn. 1997. *Resistance and conformity in the Third Reich.* London: Routledge.

Isaac of Stella. 1975. "Sermon 51." In *A short breviary,* ed. Monks of Saint John's Abbey. 4th ed. Collegeville, MN: Saint John's Abbey Press.

James, William. 1999. *The varieties of religious experience: A study in human nature.* New York: Modern Library.

Jefferson, Thomas. 2006. *The essential Jefferson.* Ed. Jean M. Yarbrough. Indianapolis: Hackett.

Kant, Immanuel. 1964. *Groundwork of the metaphysic of morals.* Trans. H.J. Paton. New York: Harper Torchbooks.

Kant, Immanuel. 1991. *Kant: Political writings.* 2nd ed. Ed. Hans Reiss. Cambridge: Cambridge University Press.

Khaled, Amr. 2006. "Message to the world regarding the Danish cartoons." <http://vb.islam2all.com/showthread.php/archive/%3Cbr%20/showthread.php?t=1373>.

Klemperer, Victor. 1998. *I will bear witness.* Trans. Martin Chalmers. New York: Random House.

Koestler, Arthur. 1964. *Darkness at noon.* Harmondsworth: Penguin.

Kosmin, Barry, and Egon Mayer. 2001. *American religious identification survey, 2001.* <http://www.egonmayer.com/emayer_aris.pdf>.

Kuhn, Thomas. 1970. *The structure of scientific revolutions.* 2nd ed. Chicago: University of Chicago Press.

Küng, Hans. 1977. *On being a Christian.* Trans. Edward Quinn. London: Collins.

Küng, Hans. 1981. *Does God exist? An answer for today.* Trans. Edward Quinn. New York: Vintage.

Lakatos, Imre. 1970. "Falsification and the methodology of scientific research programmes." In *Criticism and the growth of knowledge,* ed. Imre Lakatos and Alan Musgrave. Cambridge: Cambridge University Press.

Lane, Robert. 1991. *The market experience.* Cambridge: Cambridge University Press.

Lane, Robert. 2000. *The loss of happiness in market democracies.* New Haven: Yale University Press.

Layard, Richard. 2003. "Happiness: Has social science a clue?" Lionel Robbins Memorial Lectures. <http://www.lse.ac.uk/publicEvents/pdf/20030310t0946z003.pdf>.

Leacock, Stephen. 1989. *Arcadian adventures with the idle rich*. Toronto: McClelland & Stewart.

Lenin, V.I. 1968. *Lenin on politics and revolution*. Ed. James E. Conner. Indianapolis: Bobbs-Merrill.

Leo XIII. 1888. *Libertas Praestantissimum*. <http://www.vatican.va/holy_father/leo_xiii/encyclicals/documents/hf_l-xiii_enc_20061888_libertas_en.html>.

Lewis, Bernard. 2003. *The crisis of Islam*. New York: Modern Library.

Lewis, C.S. 1970. "The humanitarian theory of punishment." In *God in the dock*, ed. Walter Hooper. Grand Rapids, MI: William B. Eerdmans.

Lewis, C.S. 1977. *Mere Christianity*. Glasgow: Collins.

Lovejoy, Arthur O. 1964. *The Great Chain of Being: A study of the history of an idea*. Cambridge: Harvard University Press.

Lukacs, John. 1999. *Five days in London: May 1940*. New Haven: Yale University Press.

Luther, Martin. 1956. *The Sermon on the Mount*. Ed. Jaroslav Pelikan. Luther's Works, vol. 21. St Louis: Concordia Publishing House.

Luther, Martin. 1958. *Lectures on Genesis*. Ed. Jaroslav Pelikan. Luther's Works, vol. 1. St Louis: Concordia Publishing House.

Luther, Martin. 1974. *First Lectures on the Psalms*. Ed. Hilton Oswald. Luther's Works, vol. 10. St Louis: Concordia Publishing House.

Lynn, Jonathan, and Antony Jay. 1989. *The complete Yes Prime Minister*. London: BBC Books.

MacIntyre, Alasdair. 1984. *After virtue*. 2nd ed. Notre Dame: University of Notre Dame Press.

MacIntyre, Alasdair. 1988. *Whose justice? Which rationality?* Notre Dame: University of Notre Dame Press.

MacIntyre, Alasdair. 1992. "Utilitarianism and cost-benefit analysis." In *The moral dimensions of public policy choice: Beyond the market paradigm*, ed. John Gillroy and Maurice Wade. Pittsburgh: University of Pittsburgh Press.

MacIntyre, Alasdair. 1994. "A partial response to my critics." In *After MacIntyre: Critical perspectives on the work of Alasdair MacIntyre*, ed. Susan Mendus and John Horton. Notre Dame: University of Notre Dame Press.

MacIntyre, Alasdair. 2006. "Epistemological crises, dramatic narrative, and the philosophy of science." In *The tasks of philosophy*. Cambridge: Cambridge University Press.

Mandeville, Bernard. 1732. *The fable of the bees*. London: J. Tonson.

Marx, Karl, and Frederick Engels. 1942. *Selected correspondence: 1846–1895*. New York: International Publishers.

Marx, Karl, and Frederick Engels. 1969. *Selected works in three volumes*. Moscow: Progress Publishers.

Marx, Karl, and Frederick Engels. 1976. *The German ideology*. Moscow: Progress Publishers.

Maslow, Abraham. 1987. "A theory of human motivation." In *Classics of public administration*, ed. Jay. M. Shafritz and J. Steven Ott. 2nd ed. Chicago: The Dorsey Press.

McGrath, Alister, and Joanna Collicutt McGrath. 2007. *The Dawkins delusion: Atheist fundamentalism and the denial of the divine*. Downers Grove, IL: IVP Books.

Melito of Sardis. 1999. "Homily on the Passover." In *Adoration: Eucharistic texts and prayers throughout church history*, ed. Daniel Guernsey. San Francisco: Ignatius Press.

Metzger, Bruce. 1965. *The New Testament: Its background, growth, and content*. Nashville: Abingdon Press.

Mill, J.S. 1873. *The positive philosophy of Auguste Comte*. New York: Henry Holt and Co.

Mill, J.S. 1974. *On liberty*. Harmondsworth: Penguin.

Mohler, R. Albert. 2008. *Atheism Remix: A Christian confronts the New Atheists*. Wheaton, IL: Crossway Books.

Moore, David W. 2005. "American Catholics revere pope, disagree with some major teachings." *Gallup News Service*, 4 April.

Myers, David G. 1975. "Discussion-induced attitude polarization." *Human Relations* 28 (8): 699–714.

Myers, David G. 2008. *A friendly letter to skeptics and atheists*. San Francisco: Jossey-Bass.

Neurath, Otto. 1973. *Empiricism and sociology*. Ed. Marie Neurath and Robert S. Cohen. Boston: D. Reidel.

Niebuhr, Reinhold. 1960. *Moral man and immoral society*. New York: Charles Scribner's Sons.

Nietzsche, Friedrich. 1968. *The will to power*. Trans. Walter Kaufmann and R.J. Hollingdale. New York: Vintage Books.

Nietzsche, Friedrich. 1974. *The gay science*. Trans. Walter Kaufmann. New York: Vintage Books.

Nietzsche, Friedrich. 2004. *Thoughts out of season: Part one*. Trans. Anthony Ludovici. Whitefish, MT: Kessinger Publishing.

Novak, Michael. 2007. *Remembering the secular age*. First Things. June/July.

Novak, Michael. 2008. *No one sees God: The dark night of atheists and believers*. New York: Doubleday.

Onfray, Michel. 2007. *In defense of atheism: The case against Christianity, Judaism, and Islam*. Trans. Jeremy Leggatt. New York: Arcade Publishing.

Origen. 1982. "Abraham's sacrifice." In *Homilies on Genesis and Exodus*, trans. Ronald E. Heine. Washington: Catholic University of America Press.

Owen, Walter. 2010. "Christopher Hitchens and Tariq Ramadan spar over the peacefulness of Islam." <http://www.vanityfair.com/online/daily/2010/10/christopher-hitchens-and-tariq-ramadan-spar-over-the-peacefulness-of-islam>.

Pape, Robert. 2003. Dying to kill us. *New York Times*, 22 September.

Parsons, Keith. 2008. "Atheism: Twilight or dawn?" In *The future of Atheism: Alister McGrath and Daniel Dennett in dialogue*, ed. Robert B. Stewart. Minneapolis: Fortress Press.

Pascal, Blaise. 1972. *Pensées*. Paris: Le Livre de Poche.

Pinker, Steven. 2002. *The blank slate: The modern denial of human nature*. New York: Viking.

Pius XII. 1943. "Divino Afflante Spiritu." <http://www.vatican.va/holy_father/pius_xii/encyclicals/documents/hf_p-xii_enc_30091943_divino-afflante-spiritu_en.html>.

Pius XII. 1945. "Text of Pope Pius XII's address to the Sacred College of Cardinals." *New York Times*, 3 June.

Pius XII. 1950. *Humani Generis*. <http://www.vatican.va/holy_father/pius_xii/encyclicals/documents/hf_p-xii_enc_12081950_humani-generis_en.html>.

Plantinga, Alvin. 2009. "Naturalism 'ad absurdum.'" In *God is great, God is good*, ed. William Lane Craig and Chad Meister. Downers Grove, IL: InterVarsity Press.

Plato. 1959. "Euthyphro." In *The last days of Socrates*. Ed. Harold Tarrant. Harmondsworth: Penguin.

Plato. 1968. *The republic*. Trans. A. Bloom. New York: Basic Books.

Plato. 1987. "Hippias Major." In *Early Socratic dialogues*, ed. Trevor Saunders. Harmondsworth: Penguin.

Polanyi, Karl. 1957. *The great transformation*. Boston: Beacon Press.

Polanyi, Michael. 1962. *Personal knowledge*. Chicago: University of Chicago Press.

Popper, Karl. 1963. *The open society and its enemies*. New York: Harper Torchbooks.

Popper, Karl. 2002. *The logic of scientific discovery*. London: Routledge.

Proust, Marcel. 1988a. *Du côté de chez Swann. À la recherche du temps perdu*, vol. 1. Paris: Gallimard.

Proust, Marcel. 1988b. *À l'ombre des jeunes filles en fleur. À la recherche du temps perdu*, vol. 2. Paris: Gallimard.

Proust, Marcel. 1992. *Albertine disparue. À la recherche du temps perdu*, vol. 6. Paris: Gallimard.

Putnam, Hilary. 1981. *Reason, truth, and history*. Cambridge: Cambridge University Press.

Quine, W.V.O. 1951. "Two dogmas of empiricism." *Philosophical Review* 60 (1): 20–43.

Rawls, John. 1971. *A theory of justice*. Cambridge: Harvard University Press.

Rawls, John. 1995. "Political liberalism: Reply to Habermas." *Journal of Philosophy* 92 (3): 132–80.

Rawls, John. 1996. *Political liberalism*. New York: Columbia University Press.

Rawls, John. 1997. "The idea of public reason revisited." *University of Chicago Law Review* 64 (3): 765–807.

Roach, David. 2006. "Mohler, on 'O'Reilly Factor,' discusses Islam, demonic power.' *Baptist Press*, 20 March.

Rorty, Richard. 1999. *Philosophy and social hope*. London: Penguin.

Rorty, Richard. 2003. "Religion in the public square: A reconsideration." *Journal of Religious Ethics* 31 (1): 141–9.

Rousseau, Jean-Jacques. 1966. *Émile*. Paris: Garnier-Flammarion.

Rousseau, Jean-Jacques. 1972. *Les Confessions*. Paris: Librairie Générale Française.

Russell, Bertrand. 1957. "Has religion made useful contributions to civilization?" In *Why I am not a Christian, and other essays on religion and related subjects*, ed. Paul Edwards. New York: Touchstone.

Russell, Bertrand. 1997. *Religion and science*. Oxford: Oxford University Press.

Ryan, Phil. 2010. *Multicultiphobia*. Toronto: University of Toronto Press.

Ryan, Phil. 2014 (forthcoming). "Stout, Rawls, and the idea of public reason." *Journal of Religious Ethics*.

Samuelson, Paul. 1976. *Economics*. 10th ed. New York: McGraw-Hill.

Santorum, Rick. 2012. "Interview by George Stephanopoulos." *Tampa Bay Times*, 27 February.

Sartre, Jean-Paul. 1970. *L'existentialisme est un humanisme*. Paris: Nagel.

Schumacher, E.F. 1974. *Small is beautiful*. London: Abacus.

Sen, Amartya. 2009. *The idea of justice*. Cambridge: Harvard University Press.

Shakespeare, William. 1988. *The annotated Shakespeare*. Ed. A.L. Rowse. New York: Greenwich House.

Shapiro, Samantha. 2006. "Ministering to the upwardly mobile Muslim." *New York Times*, 30 April.

Smith, Adam. 1937. *The wealth of nations*. New York: Modern Library.

Smith, Adam. 2009. *Theory of moral sentiments*. London: Penguin.

Smith, Richard. 1968. "Inspiration and inerrancy." In *The Jerome Biblical commentary*, ed. Raymond Brown, Joseph Fitzmyer, and Roland Murphy. Englewood Cliffs, NJ: Prentice-Hall.

Speer, Albert. 1970. *Inside the Third Reich*. Trans. Richard and Clara Winston. New York: Macmillan.

Spinoza, Benedictus. 1992. *The ethics; Treatise on the emendation of the intellect; Selected letters*. Ed. Seymour Feldman. Indianapolis: Hackett Publishing.

Stoner, James. 2006. "Theology as knowledge." *First Things*, May.

Stout, Jeffrey. 2004. *Democracy and tradition*. Princeton: Princeton University Press.

Stratton, Jim. 2006. "Rep. Harris condemns separation of church, state." *Washington Post*, 26 August.

Swift, Jonathan. 1985. *Gulliver's travels, and other writings*. New York: Modern Library.

Sykes, J.B., ed. 1976. *Concise Oxford dictionary*. 6th ed. London: Oxford University Press.

Tawney, R.H. 1954. *Religion and the rise of capitalism*. New York: Mentor Books.

Taylor, Charles. 1989. *Sources of the self*. Cambridge: Harvard University Press.

Taylor, Charles. 1995. *Philosophical arguments*. Cambridge: Harvard University Press.

Taylor, Charles. 1999. "Democratic exclusion (and its remedies?)." In *Citizenship, diversity, and pluralism: Canadian and comparative perspectives*, ed. Alan C. Cairns. Montreal: McGill-Queen's University Press.

Taylor, Charles. 2007. *A secular age*. Cambridge: Belknap Press.

Taylor, Shelley E., and Jonathon D. Brown. 1988. "Illusion and well-being: A social psychological perspective on mental health." *Psychological Bulletin* 103 (2): 193–210.

Thucydides. 1954. *The Peloponnesian war*. Trans. R. Warner. Harmondsworth: Penguin.

Tillich, Paul. 1948. *The Protestant era*. Trans. James Luther Adams. Chicago: University of Chicago Press.

Tillich, Paul. 1952. *The courage to be*. New Haven: Yale University Press.

Times of London. 1930. "Stahlhielm rally at Coblenz." *The Times*, 7 October.

Times of London. 1933a. "German Catholics and Nazis." *The Times*, 30 March.

Times of London. 1933b. "Satisfaction in Berlin." *The Times*, 10 July.

Tocqueville, Alexis. 1986. *De la démocratie en Amérique*. Paris: Gallimard.

Tocqueville, Alexis. 1988a. *De la colonie en Algérie*. Brussels: Éditions Complexe.

Tocqueville, Alexis. 1988b. *L'ancien régime et la révolution*. Paris: Flammarion.

Townsend, Joseph. 1817. *Dissertation on the poor laws*. London: Ridgways.

Underhill, John. 1638. *Newes from America*. University of Nebraska Electronic Texts in American Studies. <http://digitalcommons.unl.edu/cgi/viewcontent.cgi?article=1037&context=etas>.

US Census Bureau. 2000. *The changing shape of the nation's income distribution, 1947–98*. <http://www.census.gov/prod/2000pubs/p60-204.pdf>.

Vassilikos, Vassilis. 1996. Z. Trans. Marilyn Calmann. New York: Four Walls Eight Windows.

Vickers, Geoffrey. 1965. *The art of judgment*. London: Chapman & Hall.

Voegelin, Eric. 1952. *The new science of politics*. Chicago: University of Chicago Press.

Walmsley, Roy. 2008. "World prison population list." 8th ed. London: International Centre for Prison Studies. <http://www.prisonstudies.org/sites/prisonstudies.org/files/resources/downloads/wppl-8th_41.pdf>.

Ward, Keith. 2007. *Is religion dangerous?* Grand Rapids, MI: William B. Eerdmans.

Washington Post. 2005. "Team Jesus Christ." *Washington Post*, 4 June.

Weber, Max. 1958. *From Max Weber: Essays in sociology*. Trans. H.H. Gerth and C. Wright Mills. New York: Oxford University Press.

Weber, Max. 2003. *The Protestant ethic and the spirit of capitalism*. New York: Dover.

Wells, Herbert George. 1901. *Anticipations of the reaction of mechanical and scientific progress upon human life and thought*. New York: Harper & Brothers.

Wieseltier, Leon. 2006. "The God Genome, review of Breaking the Spell, by Daniel Dennett." *New York Times*, 19 February.

Wolf, Hubert. 2010. *Pope and Devil: The Vatican's archives and the Third Reich*. Trans. Kenneth Kronenberg. Cambridge: Belknap Press.

Wolterstorff, Nicholas. 2008. *Justice: Rights and wrongs*. Princeton: Princeton University Press.

Woolf, Virginia. 1989. *A room of one's own*. San Diego: Harcourt.

Wright, Lawrence. 2006. *The looming tower: Al-Qaeda and the road to 9/11*. New York: Alfred A. Knopf.

Wynne, Kathleen. 2008. "Letter to Ken O'Day."<http://files.efc-canada.net/si/Education/Letter_from_OME_2008_re_Accomm.pdf>.

Zeno of Verona. 1975. "Job prefigured Christ." In *A short breviary*, ed. Monks of Saint John's Abbey. 4th ed. Collegeville, MN: Saint John's Abbey Press.